HEART LANGUAGE

Let's communicate like Jesus
and change the world!

Randy Dignan

RIVER BIRCH PRESS

Daphne, Alabama

ISBN 978-1-951561-53-6   (Print)
    978-1-951561-54-3   (Ebook)

For Worldwide Distribution
Printed in the U.S.A.
                    River Birch Press
                    P.O. Box 868
                    Daphne, AL 36526

Contents

Acknowledgments

To author this book, I have had to observe heart language in action. At this time may I thank those who have shown me what Heart Language is all about.

To my football coaches Sam Harp and Bernard Brant, thank you for the heart you taught me to leave on the field of football action and now the field of life.

To my many teachers and professors who made a difference in my life.

To my first pastor Jim Kline and your family... You all changed my life!

To Rhonda Rhea, author extraordinaire, for challenging me to put life in print.

To Mike and Judy Lewis, my in-laws, for loving my wife and teaching me Heart Language. I am so thankful for you both!

To my many preacher friends across the country who have loved me and encouraged me all these years... You have ministered to me and many others with Heart Language...

Thank you, Brian Bussey, Luke Bishop, Dave Bishop, Johnny Pope, and Rick Koonce...

To Bible Baptist Church, my first and only church. At 22 years old, you took me in, and you loved me and have demonstrated Heart Language and patience with me for almost 25 years now! I love you, church, and I thank God I am your pastor and, more so, your friend!

To the thousands of teenagers I have preached to for almost 20 years now all over the country... You all have taught me so much, and I thank God for each of you!

To Uncle Ray, who first introduced Heart language to our family! We love you and Aunt Anita and Paul, and we thank God for you all!

To my favorite brother, and favorite hearing CODA, Nick

Dignan! Words cannot express how grateful I am to have gone on this journey of life with you as my brother. I love you and I am so thankful for you and your family!

To my favorite sister and probably my biggest cheerleader Jennifer Morales... You have demonstrated Heart Language as a sister, wife, mother, and mostly as a Christian. I am so proud of you, and I love you and your family so much!

To the four children I get to hear call me Daddy! Briella, Rayana, Grant, and Clara... I am speechless and tears even fill my eyes as I utter this simple thank you! You four have been the most precious gifts God could have given your mother and me. I love you four more than you will ever know, and I am so proud to be your dad! Thank you for loving me and for teaching me Heart Language.

To the love of my life and truly my best friend! Janelle, you have been the most amazing wife a man could ever dream to have. You have stood by me, supported me, loved me, and taught me Heart Language in how you live and more importantly in who you are... I love you more each day and thank God for you!

Dad and Mom... This book says it all! Heart Language was first taught to me by you both! Everything I am today, I owe to you both. I thank God for you both, and I love you both!

Jesus, my Lord and Savior... You demonstrated Heart Language along with God the Father and the Blessed Holy Spirit... I owe my life to You! You saved me, love me, teach me, and Heart Language is now available to all because of You! Thank You!

Finally, thank you, the reader of this book, for desiring Heart Language by purchasing and reading this book. May we go on this journey together of changing the world because of... Heart Language!

Foreword

I just finished reading Randy Dignan's enlightening book, *Heart Language*. I have known and loved this young man for several years now. My introduction to Randy was over twenty years ago when the most prodigal young man in our youth group said, "Pastor, you've got to listen to this sermon! I heard him at youth camp! You're going to love him!" I did indeed listen to the sermon, and I enjoyed what he said and the way he said it. Years later, I got to know Randy. I love not only what he says and the way he says things, I love Randy! You will too, once you get to meet him. I can think of no better way of meeting one of America's finest preachers than for you to read his book.

Heart Language is an amazing book! I wept my way through the pages. Randy opened my eyes to a world I knew little about, i.e., the world of the deaf culture. The personal stories he intersperses with his message are deeply moving. I never knew the challenges, the hurts, or the blessings of this ubiquitous culture. I now feel as though I know Art and Joyce Dignan, Randy's parents, two highly educated geniuses, deaf to the world but hearing God's voice very clearly. These two were Randy's first teachers of heart language. I can honestly say that while reading the book, I heard the inimitable voice of my Savior through their Christian lives.

Randy Dignan did something else—he wove the concept of speaking and listening with one's heart by making it practical through nine different mediums. We see how the heart will affect the home, one's honesty, in humility, with happiness, in hope, blending harmony, even through the heavy things in life, guided by heroes, and finally, as Randy says, culminating in the heavenly language that leads others to Christ.

My prayer is that this book will be as much a blessing to you as it has been to me.

Yours Through Heart Language,
Johnny Pope

Preface
Language and Culture

This important section of this book lays the groundwork for the chapters to come. I was privileged to experience language and culture squared: A hearing boy born into a home with deaf parents and the deaf world; a boy who would get his education in the hearing world of public schools; a boy who would play sports all his life in the hearing world. That's what my life was, in short. Yes, I grew up experiencing both the deaf world and the hearing world.

What does that mean? The word "world" consists mainly of two parts: language and culture. Language is the main mode of communication for a community, nation, or geographical area. Culture is summed up as the behaviors, beliefs, and characteristics of a group. Most people reading this book have probably never even thought about a culture like the deaf.

My own wife of twenty-two years met only one deaf family prior to meeting mine. Now she has seen and met hundreds if not thousands of deaf, is fluent in American Sign Language, and is now quite familiar with the culture. I remember warning her of this amazing deaf culture she was about to immerse herself into. Originally my wife thought it couldn't be much different from the hearing culture. She found out quickly that yes, there is a deaf culture, and oh my is it different!

You may ask what this has to do with Jesus and what was said about Him by the officers. The point is that Jesus was cross cultural in His work while on earth. You see, while most of this world allows their cultural differences to divide them, Jesus was able to unite different cultures. Cultures are different in so many ways. They differ in appearance. They differ in clothing, and climate has a lot to do with that. Cultures differ in philosophies, in education, in background and upbringing. They differ in religion, communication, marriage, and child rearing. Cultures even differ in food!

I have eaten balut in the Philippines, tried poutine in Canada, and tasted the sweet switcha (lemonade) of the Bahamas. Food and how we eat it is unique across cultures all around the world. I could go on and on. It is quite sad that we allow our differences in culture to immediately divide us and shut down any openness to learning and exposure. I learned early on to realize that there is more that unites us than divides us.

I have also learned of the many similarities among the different cultures of the world. We all cry. We all laugh. We all hurt. We all grow old, experience emotional highs and lows, and have victories and failures. We have babies and watch them grow up. We get sick, eat, sleep, drink water, and, uh, use the restroom. We all want to be loved. We all even want to love. Hurt and pain are not respecters of culture. People in China suffer loss, people in Canada want to be loved, people in Germany want some attention, people in the Bahamas want to know somebody cares, and people in the United States of America need encouragement.

This is what made Jesus so special. Two thousand years after He left earth, His message lives on. People still sing about Him. People gather by the millions week in and week out to hear teaching about Him. People try to emulate his actions on a daily basis. Books by the thousands have been written about Him. Thousands upon thousands of sermons and messages have been presented about Him. He is the centerpiece of many a wedding. He is talked about by His critics and skeptics. Even the secular world acknowledges there was something different and maybe even special about Him.

So, what made Him so special? Here is the answer and what this book will delve into. While many people focus on our differences and barriers, Jesus was able to focus on what unites us. This goes back to the purpose of this section. Before we launch out and explain the concept of Heart Language, we must first recognize some foundational truths that will guide our thoughts. Language differences are a big barrier. I know that.

Having grown up fluent in both American Sign Language and English and living in both worlds, I have seen the barriers first-hand. You see, I spent many a day trying to bridge both worlds. My deaf parents lived in a predominantly hearing world. Everywhere my parents went outside of our home was the hearing world. The hearing world speaks a language much different than the language of the deaf.

These same differences apply in all cultures worldwide. I could walk into my house, and all of a sudden my American Sign Language communication mode clicked on. Then I would leave and go to school where all day I would speak and listen in English. The common languages of the day in which Jesus lived were Aramaic, Hebrew, Latin, and Koine Greek. However, He was able to reach and connect with all cultures.

Jesus wasn't only multilingual; He was multicultural. You ask how any of us can be that way, with the ability to communicate in a language understood by an infant, a child, a teenager, an adult, and even the senior citizen in a nursing home knocking on heaven's door. Heart Language!

You see, Mandarin, Spanish, English, French, Russian, Hebrew, and yes, even sign language are all expressed vocally, physically, and with pen and paper. In other words, these languages are written, read, spoken, and heard. Then they are understood by the intellectual side of the mind. Jesus had that ability as well. He was a great communicator, like the great communicators we all have known.

Having said that, what would lead the officers to say, "Never man spake like this man." Jesus spoke and communicated intellectually in the necessary language of His day. The difference is found in how He communicated. This will be explained in chapter one in much more depth. Jesus mastered how He spoke so that what He said was received.

Having grown up in two worlds and two cultures with two very different languages, I have learned that language isn't understood only by the mind. Language can also be heard with the heart. However, if one wants listeners to hear with their heart, then the speakers and presenters should master the art of speaking from their heart.

What language did Jesus speak in His day? Koine Greek? Aramaic? Hebrew? Even Latin? All of the above? That's what most believe. Many spoke those languages in the days of Jesus, but what He mastered was the ability to speak Heart Language. He communicated in a way that still changes lives today.

Introduction

I knew from a young age that life was different for me. You see, when I said, "Daddy, Mommy!" I heard no footsteps coming. No doors opened and closed because Mom and Dad were on their way. I could raise my voice and call their names all I wanted, but Mom and Dad wouldn't come to me. I had to go to them. I had to find them.

Why? Because my mom and dad were different than everybody else's parents. My mom and dad are deaf. They have never heard me say, "Mom! Dad!" I have never heard my parents speak to me in an intelligible voice. They spoke to me all my life but with voices they would not willingly use in public. Why? Because my dad has been deaf from birth and Mom since she was one year old. I experienced a much different upbringing than "normal."

I had quite a different experience from all my peers, contemporaries, and friends. My grandparents were deaf, and my great-grandparents as well. I also have deaf aunts, uncles, and cousins. I remember when I was six years old and my brother (who could hear) was four, we were informed that our baby sister who was one year old had just lost her hearing.

Fast-forward many years later, and my adult deaf sister is now married to a deaf man with a deaf daughter, twin hard-of-hearing sons, and an infant hearing son. Life has for sure been different for my brother and me. I share all this not to seek sympathy. You see, I loved it! I grew up bilingual and bicultural. However, beyond that, my bilingual and bicultural experiences were different than that of many others who grew up bilingual and bicultural. Why?

Because the deaf world has some unique aspects regarding language and culture. It is commonly known that the deaf world and deaf culture is the only known culture without a native homeland. Why again? Because every country has deaf people who live in their country. The deaf culture uses a visual language that is seen, rather than heard, spoken, or written. So, my journey was radical and my learning experiences unique, and boy did I learn some things that most people don't!

I was the firstborn in my family, so according to my parents, my native language is ASL (American Sign Language). It has been said that if you know three languages, you are trilingual. If you know two languages, you are bilingual. If you know one language, you are American. What does this have to do with anything?

Enter Jesus and this amazing verse in the Bible:

> *The officers answered, Never man spake like this man* (John 7:46).

What did the officers mean? What is the real meaning of this statement? Jesus obviously wasn't speaking a different language. He wasn't going back and forth between languages or speaking gibberish. He clearly wasn't speaking to impress. What was the difference? The Pharisees had sent the officers to arrest Jesus. Here are more verses to lay the groundwork for this truth.

> *Many of the people therefore, when they heard this saying, said, Of a truth this is the Prophet. Others said, This is the Christ. But some said, Shall Christ come out of Galilee?*
>
> *Hath not the scripture said, That Christ cometh of the seed of David, and out of the town of Bethlehem, where David was? So there was a division among the people because of him.*
>
> *And some of them would have taken him; but no man laid hands on him. Then came the officers to the chief priests and Pharisees; and they said unto them, Why have ye not brought him? The officers answered, Never man spake like this man. Then answered them the Pharisees, Are ye also deceived?* (John 7:40–47)

Jesus had been teaching and preaching. So had many others. The Pharisees spoke regularly, the prophets had been speaking for years, and so had the chief priests and Sadducees. The Pharisees and chief priests had arranged Jesus' arrest. He was to be brought before the Pharisees because He was, in their mind, stirring up trouble, teaching things they thought were contrary to what they believed. When all was said and done, they were just jealous!

That led to the statement, "Never man spake like this man." This statement the officers uttered is the theme of this book. As we explore what they were saying and teaching generations to come without realizing it, let us learn what they unintentionally taught all of us in their statement.

The "way" Jesus spoke was so powerful that in only a few minutes of conversation, the officers made an observation about Jesus that can change our lives for the better. This truth can help a father as he speaks to his children. This truth can help the employer address issues with an employee in such a way that the employee will work harder and be more productive. This truth can help thousands of pastors, preachers, and missionaries all over the world be more effective every time they step into a pulpit. This truth can help politicians and even the president as they speak to their constituency on a regular basis. This truth, when utilized daily, can encourage even a stranger. So, get ready, here we go! Let's learn Heart Language!

Let's learn how to communicate. Let's learn Heart Language. Let's change our world. Let's change the entire world. Let's change HOW we communicate starting right now.

One

Communication Changes the World

The officers answered, Never man spake like this man
(John 7:46).

It was 1983. I still remember this day like it was yesterday.
I was eight years old, and I was in the third grade. This day I
woke up a little more nervous than any other day. Today was
the day my class was going to put on a program for our parents.

This program was to take place in the latter part of the
afternoon so that parents could work out their schedules to
be there and watch their children perform. We had practiced
for weeks, and today was the big day! Most of my classmates
were nervous for a different reason than I was.

You see, because the year was 1983 and not 1990 yet,
none of the changes 1990 brought had begun. In that year,
the Americans with Disabilities Act (ADA) was passed and
became law. This law would grant people with disabilities
equal access to the many necessary services provided to the
majority.

Examples include wheelchair ramps and elevators for wheelchair users, better accommodations for persons with visual impairments, and of course readily available sign language interpreting for persons with hearing loss across the country. The deaf world has seen huge strides in minimalizing barriers between the deaf and hearing world. The government has helped with that, as technology has been developed to help people with hearing loss, and today you will regularly see sign language interpreters working in their communities all over the world.

But back in 1983, I was nervous. The program was definitely in the back of my mind, but my reason for being nervous was not specifically the program. I knew my parents would be attending. They had gotten the letter the teacher sent home with the students announcing the time and date of the program. I was to stand up on a platform with my classmates, singing some songs and quoting some stanzas.

Here is why I was nervous: Who would interpret for my parents? There were no interpreters. None of my classmates had parents who knew sign language. I could try to do it, but would they see me? I was taller than some of my classmates, so I always stood in the back row. But my classmates' faces and heads would block my hands even if I did try to sign. I wanted to tell my parents that they did not need to attend. I would understand. I could explain everything to them later.

The time came. The program was starting. I climbed onto the stage and scanned the crowd. There, in the back, I saw my dad and mom. Both were smiling and signing, "I love you" to me. I returned their smile. When the program started, I sang with my class and recited the stanzas, and there my parents sat, unable to understand any of it.

They knew nothing of what was being said. They did not hear the instruments or the song. They had no clue what the program was about. Yet there they sat, smiling. My father was an educator with two master's degrees, and my mother also was an educator with a bachelor's degree, yet they weren't able to understand anything presented by the third-grade class that day.

What still brings tears to my eyes many years later is that they knew they wouldn't be able to understand any of the program and yet they still came. Some may wonder why.

My parents, as well as many other deaf of their generation, grew up watching television and movies trying to guess story lines, plots, and endings without ever hearing the words. They would try to read lips even, and that was hardly ever accurate.

As the program continued, I kept seeing my dad and mom smiling from ear to ear. Then I could feel it coming— the quiver of my lip was starting. See, I've always been a crier. There came the waterworks! My classmates began to look at me out the corners of their eyes. My teacher was also noticing me with concern.

This was not part of the program. Parents in the audience viewed me with concern as well. I am sure many thought that day that I was experiencing a dose of stage fright. Maybe they thought my nerves had gotten the best of me. I mean, the children in my class were only in the third grade, only eight, maybe nine years old. They did not know why I was crying, and they would never know. Even if I had told them, they wouldn't have understood anyway. It was OK. I got it. It was not their fault.

Ignorance is not always a bad or negative word. You can't

be angry or get frustrated when people don't understand a certain situation. Two people in the crowd that day knew full well why this eight-year-old boy was crying. I call them Dad and Mom. They understood, but they were going to be there anyway! Why? Because they loved their son and wanted me to be sure I knew it.

This was a significant day for me. Although I am sure I had many opportunities to recognize Heart Language prior to this day, at that moment I truly recognized it. I am forty-four years old at the time of this writing. I have been married for twenty-two years and am the father of four children. This lesson still resonates in my mind and especially in my heart. Acts of love and demonstrations of genuine care truly do leave lasting impressions. For it was on this day, as an eight-year-old third grader, that I realized I was being taught my third and most important language for life: Heart Language.

I like the English language, and I love American Sign Language, but Heart Language has truly changed my life. That day I became a student of Heart Language without even realizing it. Class was in session. Lessons were being distributed. I entered the school of Heart Language, and I had two of the best instructors a student could ask for. I called him Dad. I called her Mom.

Jesus and Heart Language

Now we see what set Jesus apart. Everybody was important to Him. The children loved Him. The rejected flocked to Him. The lonely followed Him. The hurting sought out a comforting word. The sick needed healing. The hurting needed some salve for their soul. The hungry wanted but a morsel of satisfaction. The weary wanted a pillow. The sad

4

needed uplifting. The frustrated needed to be told it was going to be OK. The brokenhearted wanted a touch. The sinner needed hope. The abused needed compassion. The lost needed to be found.

What drives the man who wants to attempt to meet those needs? Halls of education and all their degrees and diplomas are good but do not teach this lesson. Governments all over the world who bicker and fuss over their many petty disagreements don't always grasp this concept. The work force many times is consumed with the bottom line. The businessman is determined to expand and grow. The pastor has checked his attendance once again and is not happy with the numbers. We must grow and we must build. Bigger and better is what we strive for, always.

None of these things are necessarily wrong, but what if, just what if . . . we actually began to lead, preach, teach, and communicate with Heart Language. This world is hurting and in many ways is lost. Let's break down the three main components of communication and see what it was about Jesus that confirmed He was a master of Heart Language.

The Who

*Many **of the people** therefore, when **they heard** this saying, said, Of a truth this is the Prophet. Others said, This is the Christ. But some said, Shall Christ come out of Galilee?*

*Hath not the scripture said, That Christ cometh of the seed of David, and out of the town of Bethlehem, where David was? So there was a division **among the people** because of him.*

*And **some of them** would have taken him; but no man laid hands on him. Then came the officers to the chief priests and Pharisees; and they said unto them, Why have ye not brought him? **The officers** answered, Never man spake like this man. Then answered them the Pharisees, Are ye also deceived?* (John 7:40–47)

I call your attention to the words in bold. These represent the "whos" of this particular passage. We don't often take into consideration the many whos we communicate with every day. I understand that not every conversation has to be vetted through the potential filter of Heart Language, but I do believe this world can use a whole lot more Heart Language and not less.

The stage is set in this passage. Jesus is teaching again. He is presenting His truth to a crowd of observers who are giving Him an audience. Jesus in His wisdom knows this crowd consists of different groups of listeners. Some are there to learn. Some are hoping for another miracle. Some simply had nothing else to do. Some were waiting for the right time to challenge Him or critique Him as before.

Finally, some were there for one reason and one reason alone—to arrest Him! Jesus knew these things. He knew the content was important and even controversial. What separated Jesus from so many of His day is that He always put the who at the forefront of His mind. His audience was as important as the truth He wanted to convey. Heart Language helps us communicate to all the whos of our life.

Take a moment now and think about your whos. Daily, our whos are made up of a spouse, a child, a coworker, a boss, a clerk at a store, a parent, a pastor, a fellow church member, a business partner, a doctor, a dentist—we could go on and on. Life is interesting because of the many whos in our lives.

Too many times in our lives we place ourselves in a box and expect so much conformity in how we live, think, and even communicate. We should be so thankful God made us all so different. We have unique backgrounds, personalities, attitudes, outlooks, goals, and desires. This is what makes the world so special and amazing.

Jesus knew this! He knew his audiences and crowds were made up of the young, the old, Jewish, Roman, upper class, the poor, men, women, and the list goes on. Our whos of life are sometimes one-on-one relationships, as in a small group, a meeting at work, or even a congregation at church. In other words, the whos make the world go around. What would life be like without everybody else? Imagine that for a moment!

Who we communicate with daily is something we take for granted. So many casual conversations take place with people we know well and don't know so well all the time. In conversing, we learn things, we establish schedules, and we draw closer. Think about your best friend right now and think back to the first conversation you had with him or her. Your friendship had to start somewhere.

I love to study how Jesus interacted with the different groups of whos He had in His life. He had to communicate with family, His disciples, the Pharisees, the Romans, the Gentiles, the masses, the children, and even the Samaritans. The whos of our life are many times consistent and constant. We see regular whos every day, and we talk to them and share information. We also know that unfortunately it is the whos we love the most that sometimes we hurt the most. As we learn communication that can change the world, let's next look at what we say.

The What

> *Many of the people therefore, when they heard this saying, said, Of a truth this is the Prophet.*
>
> *Then came the officers to the chief priests and Pharisees; and they said unto them, Why have ye not brought him? The officers answered, Never man spake like this man. Then answered them the Pharisees, Are ye also deceived?* (John 7:40, 45–47).

What Jesus said was so vital. What Jesus came to say on earth was and is life changing and even eternal. He had massive audiences. He spoke to the multitude. He spoke to His disciples when He knew others were within earshot.

He spoke to many people one-on-one. You will find that true in John 3, 4, 5, 8, and 9 as well as other instances in the Gospels. What He said to Nicodemus differed from what He said to the woman at the well, and that differed from what He said to the blind man and many others. Jesus had a purpose for all His "whats" that He shared with His many different "whos."

Daily, we share many whats. What time is a child's practice? What time are we meeting? Who is picking up the kids after school? What do you want to eat tonight? We also encounter more serious whats like, how did your mom's surgery go? Did you hear the boss is sick? We need to meet. Your work has been slipping lately. Please meet me in my office.

Even in our passage above, note that "of a truth" is mentioned as well as the question, "Are ye also deceived?" Why would they ask that? Deceived by what? Exactly! The Pharisees were asking if the officers had been deceived by what Jesus said. Introduce . . .

The How

The officers answered, Never man spake like this man. Then answered them the Pharisees, Are ye also deceived? (John 7:46–47)

This is the section I am most excited about—the how! Let's go back to the start of this chapter. It was 1983, and my school had a program. I was concerned as an eight-year-old boy that my parents, as usual, were going to miss out on anything that required hearing to enjoy the program.

The whos were in attendance. The whats were the program itself. Why did I start to learn Heart Language that day without even realizing it? I mean, my parents would watch me in future programs and plays. They watched dozens and dozens of football games and basketball games, as well as other sporting events. That day, though—why?

Because of their "how." The same reason the officers said, "Never man spake like this man." My parents were not worried about the program. They knew it wasn't life or death if they did or didn't have an interpreter. They just wanted their eight-year-old little boy to know he was loved and that they would be there.

The how is so incredibly important. Many of our daily conversations emphasize what is said and to whom it is said without giving much thought to how it is said. When we say what we say to whom we need to say it to, without caring how we say it, often the listener remembers the how more than the actual message of the what.

Jesus introduced something so different, so powerful, and so impactful. His priority was on how He said things, and then the who He said them to, and the what He said became

9

simple. Whether we are a dad, a mom, a pastor, a teacher, a preacher, a boss, a supervisor, a politician, or any type of leader, how we say what we say makes a huge difference.

In other words, when what we say becomes the priority and not the how, the who will remember the how more than the what. When we focus on our how, the who will listen better to the what. On that 1983 day in my school, what my parents did was so powerful, they did not even have to say a word.

What did the officers mean by their simple observation? Here is what they meant: His how was so powerful they couldn't arrest Him. He cared. He loved. He spoke in such a way that listeners struggled, debating His what because His how was full of love and sincerity. It's the old saying that states, "People don't care how much you know until they know how much you care."

Sometimes the how is in your tone or your inflection, or it may be found in the gentleness of your eyes. We live in a world dominated by media and even social media. People hide behind keyboards and cameras and spew out mean and hateful things to people and about people they know little about.

Turn on a talk show. It starts with a subject, a what, and a bunch of whos start chatting, and then the how gets out of hand. Self-control goes out the window, anger takes over, and the what becomes the driving force of the communication rather than the how. Jesus spoke Aramaic sometimes. Jesus spoke Hebrew sometimes. Jesus spoke Koine Greek sometimes as well. However, He always spoke Heart Language.

As a man, husband, father, pastor who is fluent in American Sign Language, English, and even knows enough

Spanish to make me dangerous—may I always speak with Heart Language. As a husband, I need to use Heart Language. As a father, I need to speak with Heart Language. As a preacher, may I stand in pulpits and share messages with Heart Language.

What's amazing about this is that we can find a common denominator. Not everybody knows Spanish. Not everybody understands French. Not everybody can write Russian. Not everybody can read Mandarin. Not everybody speaks Tagalog. Not everybody can learn all the languages of the world and be fluent in them.

Good news! Everybody, no matter the language or culture of your life, can use and understand Heart Language. Heart Language is a smile. It is the wink of an eye. It may be the sound of love in a voice. It might be simply being present. Maybe it's a gentle touch. It could be sitting in a nursing home. It's the joyous sound of laughter. It's found in a kind note. It's sent as a thoughtful text. It can also be a simple, "How do you do?" It's the gift of a flower. For sure it is crying with someone.

It's making that visit in a hospital. It's stopping to thank a soldier. Maybe it's paying for someone's meal. It's definitely praying with someone. To many it is a piece of chocolate for a hurting friend. In many cases it's as simple as singing off tune to make someone laugh. Heart Language can be something that comes to your mind right now.

Heart Language was evident in the life of Jesus so much so that it was declared to the powers that be "that never man spake like this man." Finally, Heart Language is when two deaf people show up at their eight-year-old son's school program even though they knew they understand nothing of it.

Why? Love! My parents were my first teachers of Heart Language, and amazing teachers they were. Let's take our journey of learning Heart Language from Jesus, as well as these two amazing people I call Dad and Mom. Let's learn Heart Language. Let's "speak" Heart Language. Let's change the world!

Two

We Can Use Help

*And ofttimes it hath cast him into the fire, and into the
waters, to destroy him: but if thou canst do any thing,
have compassion on us, and help us. Jesus said unto him, If
thou canst believe, all things are possible to him that believeth* (Mark 9:22–23).

It was opening day of school. As I walked into the classroom, I braced myself for the first roll call. I was still in elementary school, and I was starting at my fourth school
already in my short life. Many would stop me at this point
and ask if my father was military. I would politely answer no;
my father is deaf. The question made sense, however, because
why else would I be starting my fourth elementary school already?

You see, my deaf father had a unique opportunity in the
1980s. He was the rare educator who was deaf himself and
had earned a bachelor's degree plus two master's degrees. He
became a popular role model in deaf schools to show young
deaf students that they too could grow up, graduate from college, and lead successful lives.

My father's story is pretty amazing! He graduated from

the Florida School for the Deaf and Blind in the late 1950s with a second-grade reading level. His future was destined to be in blue collar work, and he was OK with that as many others were, at first. Then one day he decided he wanted something more.

He bought himself a dictionary and read through it. I mean, who does that? My dad did! Seven years after graduating high school, he went to Gallaudet College (now Gallaudet University), played football there, and eventually graduated. Oh, and he also met my mother, who was attending there after her graduation from the Ohio School for the Deaf.

Nearly every state in the United States of America has a residential school for the deaf that provides K–12 education for all persons with hearing loss. Having said that, in the 1950s, 1960s, and 1970s, education was not what it is today for the deaf. The oral method (emphasizing lip reading and speech and not sign language) was the common venue for educating the deaf. My father had to overcome these obstacles and get an education pretty much on his own, and that was a big deal in the 1980s.

Here we go! First day of school. The teacher starts to call roll. We all know how that works. Last name is called out, then the first name, followed by the student's response of here or present. A, B, C . . .

"Dignan, Randolph," said the teacher.

"That'll be Randy, ma'am. Here." The name Randy didn't get made fun of as much as Randolph. Even my own brother came up with a song called "Randolph the Red-Faced Dignan."

"OK, great! Randy it is. Wait, are you the son of the new

teacher at the deaf school in the area? I have heard of him."

"Yes, ma'am."

"Well, class. This is exciting. We have a new student, and his father is deaf. Is your mother deaf as well?"

"Yes she is. I also have a younger deaf sister."

"Wow! May I ask you a question?"

"Yes, that would be fine."

Now I feel sixty eyeballs fixated on me, belonging to thirty classmates. Oh boy, recess is going to be fun today. You see, I have never been embarrassed about my parents being deaf. Not one day of my life! However, when you have deaf parents, especially in the 1970s and 1980s and even into the 1990s, it could definitely lead to some interesting questions. I have been asked many questions that would leave many people scratching their heads. You may hear some of those questions as this book moves along.

"So, class, we may spend time this year asking Randolph, I mean Randy, questions. Won't that be great?"

Yeah, great! When can we get started?

"Randy, we do need to move on and finish taking attendance, but I must ask this question. Do you have to go grocery shopping with your mom so that you can read the price tags for her?"

I guess we are getting started now. What? Did you just ask me that question in front of my thirty classmates? How am I supposed to answer this without sounding disrespectful? I mean, a part of me wanted to say, "Are you serious? You just asked that question out loud and you are a teacher! This will be a long year."

I knew I couldn't do that. My parents taught me from a young age that many times people mean well but speak their mind or ask questions out of ignorance. Ignorance, again, is not necessarily a negative word. It just means not knowing or a lack of knowledge.

"Uh . . . no, ma'am. My mom can read price tags," I said as respectfully as I could.

"Uh . . . uh . . . oh! Of course. OK, let's move along, class," she said, blushing.

Recess was fun that day. Whenever I started at a new school, the students would always come up to me and ask me to teach them sign language. It made me popular, temporarily. Funny thing about this, though, the girls always wanted to learn signs for pretty, nice, thank you, nice to meet you, and phrases like these. The boys, however, always wanted me to teach them the swear words.

I spent much of my first recess teaching the girls and boys sign language. Well, more so the girls since they were asking signs that were good for normal conversation, and of course I did not know the signs for swear words. Well, maybe I did. I also liked teaching the girls because they were prettier. So much for showing all my new classmates how good I was at tetherball. Yes, tetherball! If you've never played tetherball on a public school playground, you've missed out.

As the day went on, I began to wonder if I should tell my parents about the question the teacher asked. Previously, I had shared questions like these with my parents, so I figured I would go ahead and share this question with them as well. I knew they would respond differently.

They would usually laugh at the absurdity of the question. Then they would realize that once again the question was asked out of ignorance. Then they would react somewhat differently. My dad would start to say that he needed to write a note to the teacher and maybe educate her about this subject and strongly encourage her to think before she asked a question in the future. When my dad "strongly encouraged" people to do things, they usually did them. My mom, on the other hand, would probably be more concerned with how it affected me.

Because of what was discussed in the previous chapter, I could easily move on. Because I knew they used Heart Language and were trying to teach it to me as well, we moved on recognizing that ignorance, and not the teacher, was the guilty culprit.

You see, the issue with me as a young child getting asked that question in front of my class was that there was no one in the room to empathize. That was OK with me because I had been conditioned up to that point to expect situations like this. The teacher was not being mean. I understood that even as a young elementary-aged child.

I also realize even to this day that it's not every day you meet a deaf person or a CODA (child of deaf adult). My parents had emphasized to me all my life that what I was experiencing as I grew up was unique, and not everybody got to have deaf parents. They were right. I chose at a young age to believe I was privileged to have deaf parents. It wasn't a burden; it was a blessing. However, with this blessing came many ignorant responses, statements, and questions.

Again, because of Heart Language, I learned early on that this ignorance can be accepted as a good challenge. I have the privilege to educate much of the general population, the majority, about this silent minority called the deaf world. Even at forty-four years old today, I am asked questions out of curiosity about my experiences. These experiences have led to newspaper articles, radio interviews, and even a four-season TV program series on a Christian television station.

The thought for this chapter, though, is "helpful language." The text from the Bible we used to make application here is found in the Book of Mark.

> *And ofttimes it hath cast him into the fire, and into the waters, to destroy him: but if thou canst do any thing, have compassion on us, and help us. Jesus said unto him, If thou canst believe, all things are possible to him that believeth* (Mark 9:22–23).

Notice the plea from the father. Let's read more of the text.

> *And when he came to his disciples, he saw a great multitude about them, and the scribes questioning with them. And straightway all the people, when they beheld him, were greatly amazed, and running to him saluted him.*
>
> *And he asked the scribes, What question ye with them? And one of the multitude answered and said, Master, I have brought unto thee my son, which hath a dumb spirit; And wheresoever he taketh him, he teareth him: and he foameth, and gnasheth with his teeth, and pineth away: and I spake to thy disciples that they should cast him out; and they could not.*
>
> *He answereth him, and saith, O faithless generation, how long shall I be with you? how long shall I suffer you? bring him unto me. And they brought him unto him: and when he saw him, straightway the spirit tare him; and he fell on the ground, and wallowed foaming. And he asked his father, How long is it ago since this came unto him?*

And he said, Of a child. And ofttimes it hath cast him into the fire, and into the waters, to destroy him: but if thou canst do any thing, have compassion on us, and help us Jesus said unto him, If thou canst believe, all things are possible to him that believeth.

And straightway the father of the child cried out, and said with tears, Lord, I believe; help thou mine unbelief.

When Jesus saw that the people came running together, he rebuked the foul spirit, saying unto him, Thou dumb and deaf spirit, I charge thee, come out of him, and enter no more into him. And the spirit cried, and rent him sore, and came out of him: and he was as one dead; insomuch that many said, He is dead.

But Jesus took him by the hand, and lifted him up; and he arose. And when he was come into the house, his disciples asked him privately, Why could not we cast him out? And he said unto them, This kind can come forth by nothing, but by prayer and fasting (Mark 9:14–29).

Wow! What a story! This story shows a father who is in desperation mode and only wants somebody to help him. How does this relate to my first day of school story and Heart Language? I am glad you asked.

In life, so many times we will come across people who are hurting and going through difficult times. In many situations, the desire to help those in need is there, but the how to is not. The reason for this is simple. What do you say to a young boy who grew up with deaf parents after he's asked an ignorant question in front of the whole class? Even more so, what do you say to a father who is suffering because of his son's situation and is in desperate need of somebody to help?

Many well-meaning people truly do want to help. I found myself many times through the years wanting to help someone hurting but simply didn't know what to say. Helpful language is an interesting language. It is a language that all cultures need and desire because of all the hurt that life can bring upon us. We know we need to help. We know we should say something. We know we should try to encourage, but how?

What does one say? How do we go about addressing this issue of a young boy singled out in front of his class, or a grieving, desperate father? That's where Heart Language kicks in. Let's look at how helpful language can literally help.

The first step to helpful language is to make sure we are beginning to understand what chapter one taught about Heart Language. Next, we need to ask questions and listen. You may be reading this as a parent, a pastor, a teacher, or even a CEO, and you may be asking how you can help your child, your church members in need, your students, or your employees.

Half of the battle is done with simply listening. Notice that Jesus hears the father out. He listens to his request. He hears the desperation. He asks a question. He understands the situation before He even addresses it. To the person you are desiring to help, it means the world to them if you just take time to listen to them. Listen to their hurt. Listen to their dilemma. Listen to their situation. Listen to their concerns. Listen to their problems.

This is why we have two ears (to listen twice as much), two eyes (to observe twice as much), and one mouth (to speak half as much). Listening to someone is helping them, and the listening becomes so much easier when you live with the mindset of Heart Language.

When I first started pastoring at twenty-two years old, hospital visits made me nervous. First of all, how sick is the person I am visiting? How well do I know them? How medically savvy am I that I might understand what they are going through? After twenty-two years of pastoring, I have learned that half of my "job" was finished when I walked into the hospital room. The majority of the rest of my job was completed by simply listening to the one in need of help. Jesus almost always got some backstory about the individuals He was helping. He genuinely showed He cared by listening to those in need of help.

We start with listening. Then we spend time trying to understand what we have heard. Here is where many people struggle. We will not always understand what we are dealing with. However, we can still show care, compassion, and love while speaking with helpful language.

When we spend the proper amount of time listening, we also reduce the risk of the greatest fear of all leaders: saying the wrong thing! How do I know that? Because I have said the wrong thing one too many times. Remember, hurting people simply want to know that someone cares and that someone wants to help.

Today, we see how social media is changing our society and relationships. People launch negative words and hurtful sentiments toward people they don't even know well, all while hiding behind a smart phone or a computer keyboard somewhere. Sometimes they even have fake accounts. They say things in the cyber world they would never have the guts to say to someone face-to-face. Helpful language understands that when all is said and done, even if I don't say a whole lot, the hurting individual can look into my eyes and know I care.

Finally, when learning to adopt helpful language into our daily lives, we must simply abide by the golden rule, which of course comes from a Bible verse spoken by Jesus Himself.

Therefore all things whatsoever ye would that men should do to you, do ye even so to them: for this is the law and the prophets (Matthew 7:12).

That's right! How many times have we been hurting? How many times have we been struggling? How many times in our lives did we feel like nobody understood how we felt? How many times did we feel like nobody is even making an effort to reach out to us? The lessons of the past can sure help us in the present to be a blessing to someone else's future. Helpful language is that powerful.

The end of the story is beautiful. Jesus heals this desperate father's son. The witnesses are amazed at how Jesus was able to help them. He teaches His own disciples a valuable lesson about helping people. This world is a much better place because of the helpers out there. It is not easy to always listen, speak, and of course live helpful language, but it is always worth it to the helped and even to the helper.

The teacher asked me a question. So what? She didn't understand. She had no knowledge at all of what it was like to grow up in a deaf home and live in a deaf world, but my father and my mother did. I was fine because when I got home where my parents lived out Heart Language and helpful language, their young son had a good laugh and remembered how privileged he was to live in this amazing and interesting world. Helpful language helped me get through this awkward situation with ease. Oh, and the class found out how good I was at tetherball in the following days.

Jesus mastered the use of helpful language, and it changed lives. We now can help, and change lives as well. Let's change the world by using helpful language.

Three

Not in a Pharmacy

Jesus went unto the mount of Olives. And early in the morning he came again into the temple, and all the people came unto him; and he sat down, and taught them. And the scribes and Pharisees brought unto him a woman taken in adultery; and when they had set her in the midst,

They say unto him, Master, this woman was taken in adultery, in the very act. Now Moses in the law commanded us, that such should be stoned: but what sayest thou? This they said, tempting him, that they might have to accuse him.

But Jesus stooped down, and with his finger wrote on the ground, as though he heard them not. So when they continued asking him, he lifted up himself, and said unto them, He that is without sin among you, let him first cast a stone at her. And again he stooped down, and wrote on the ground.

And they which heard it, being convicted by their own conscience, went out one by one, beginning at the eldest, even unto the last: and Jesus was left alone, and the woman standing in the midst.

When Jesus had lifted up himself, and saw none but

the woman, he said unto her, Woman, where are those thine accusers? hath no man condemned thee? She said, No man, Lord. And Jesus said unto her, Neither do I condemn thee: go, and sin no more (John 8:1–11).

What a passage! This may be one of my favorite passages in all the Gospels. Jesus is challenged and put on the spot when dealing with someone who has failed. Yes, that's me. That's also you. We all fail. Life is tough, and we can do our best, but we will fail and we will fall.

I have fallen many times, and I've had to get back up again. One of my favorite quotes of all time is, "Failure is an event, not a person." So many times in our lives, our workplaces, our churches, and even our homes, our failures get magnified more than necessary. Jesus, being an expert in Heart Language, also knew when to apply that to healing language. Hence, the title of this chapter, "Not in a Pharmacy."

The word "heal" is a powerful word. I love its meaning. It simply means to make healthy and to restore to health. When we think of the word, we often think of a physical injury, a sickness, or a disease. Doctors spend their whole lives healing the sick, diseased, and injured. I am so thankful for all the work, research, and study that goes into helping all of us better take care of our bodies and health. The healing of a failing heart, the healing of a broken bone, and the healing of a nasty cut still put me in awe.

However, this is not what this chapter is about. You see, we are facing a serious epidemic in the world today, and that is of a hurting heart, hurting emotions, and even a sick spirit. A hard fall in a football game may break a bone, but harsh words to a young child can wound the spirit of the child much longer. We live in a world where what we say is almost always more important than how we say it, and it's causing a lot of hurt, sadness, discouragement, and even depression. May God help us learn to speak healing language!

I remember a situation from when I was a little boy. I had gotten in trouble again. Yes, my father was not happy. One of the biggest misconceptions about growing up in a home with deaf family is the assumed silence that comes with it. Uh, no! Homes with deaf people are more noisy because the deaf individuals are not able to hear the noise they are making.

The pots banging. The doors slamming. The cupboards shutting. It's true! I can testify. Having said that, though, the same applies when they speak. They also can come across louder than normal because they can't hear their own voices and regulate the volume. Many people think deaf people can't speak. That is not true. Most deaf people are able to speak, and many do.

It's not that they can't; it's that they won't. The reason people tend to think deaf people are mute is because many of them, including my parents and sister, don't use their voices out in public. I am often asked how I learned to speak, having grown up in a deaf home. My parents used their voices at home all the time but only rarely in public. Because many deaf have never heard sound, it is more difficult for them to speak in what we would call an intelligible voice.

Since I was the firstborn in my family, I was a little bit behind as a two-year-old in my speech. My parents entered me into a preschool with three- and four-year-olds, and according to my teachers, I caught up in my speech because of my interactions with the other kids. So, I have and still hear the voices of my parents and sister when we are together at home in a casual setting, and may I say, I love their voices.

But back to my story. I was in trouble. My father was very loving but also a strict disciplinarian. (By the way, I am thankful he was both. Our country needs well-balanced fathers that are both.) I was lying in my bed because I was being disciplined. I had upset my father. I did wrong, and he was punishing me. Again, I want to make sure and emphasize that my father disciplined me the right way, and I deserved every bit of it.

As I lay on the bed this particular time, I knew I was in trouble. My little brother was already asleep. My sister was a baby at this time, so she was out in the living room with my mother. While lying there and thinking about what I had done and my punishment, I heard the footsteps of my father coming down the hallway heading to my room. The lights were off and it was dark. He pushed the door open, and the light from the hallway illuminated the room just enough for me to see him standing there. Since it was pretty dark, we would most likely not be signing to each other, so he spoke.

"Randy," my father said in a voice most would not readily understand. "I just want you to know that even though you did wrong and you disappointed me, I love you and I wouldn't trade you for a million dollars." (I have wondered if he would've traded me for two million dollars.)

I signed back in the light that was enough for him to see, "Thank you, and I love you."

"Good night," he said, and he went back down the hallway. I smiled very big, then rolled over and went right to sleep.

If my father would have said those words to any other

child my age at that time, most likely they would not have understood, but I understood my father's words loud and clear. I was healed. You see, the process of disciplining a child, or any subordinate for that matter, is never complete unless healing language is used to seal the deal. My deaf father, a user of American Sign Language all of his life, spoke English to me in that dark room that night in what we call a "deafy" voice, but I understood him loud and clear. It wasn't the sign language or the English that helped this little boy who had gotten in trouble again to smile himself to sleep that night. It was healing language. I don't know how my father and mother learned healing language, but I sure am glad they did.

In John 8, Jesus is faced with a dilemma. Here, once again, He is put on the spot. The situation is bleak for this woman. According to the Pharisees, she was caught in the very act. By the way, let's pause for a moment. If she were caught in the very act, pray tell me where the man was. Why was he not brought before Jesus as well? That is a question that goes unanswered.

Jesus is teaching the people. He is at the temple, and it is an early morning. The people have gathered to hear His wisdom. Things are going well, and then, boom! The Pharisees show up and bring a woman right into the middle of the crowd and put out their challenge. They want to see punishment. They want to see Jesus confounded. They want to make Jesus look bad.

Yes, this woman is guilty. I mean, she was caught in the very act. She now stoops in fear as many eyes gaze upon her, knowing that she is at the mercy of the Pharisees and Jesus. What is going to happen next? They pressure Jesus for a response. They want to see how He is going to handle this.

They want to see if He will be in line with Jewish tradition and Mosaic Law.

I mean, the Law states what should be done when one is caught in this act. They even remind Jesus that she is to be stoned and executed for this act. The questions ring out, "What sayest thou?" Jesus stoops to the ground. I love this part! He begins to write on the ground. The spotlight has shifted from the Pharisees and the woman to Jesus.

What would He do? Would He contradict the Law? Would He condemn this lady? Would He excuse her? Would He side with the Pharisees? Would He try to be neutral? Would He delegate the decision? The woman's life literally was in the balance! She was condemned by the Law. She was supposed to die and she knew it. What was He going to do?

His disciples were watching. The Pharisees were looking on. The people that gathered at the temple stared in wonder at what might happen next. Jesus stooped, wrote on the ground, and acted as if He didn't even hear them. Why did He stoop? Maybe He wanted to look the woman in the eye and assure her without saying a word that everything was going to be OK. The Pharisees got frustrated, and the Bible says they continued asking Him.

The Pharisees thought they had Him. The law was on their side, as well as Jewish tradition. The pressure was on, or was it? You see, nobody factored in the power of Jesus and healing language. Jesus stood back up and simply said, "He that is without sin among you, let him first cast a stone at her." He stooped down and started writing on the ground again.

Wow! What? Did Jesus just do a mic drop? Yes, He did! How can you debate this statement by Jesus? He took it all in. He observed. He was in no rush to respond. He kicked in healing language, and before the game has even started, He won, or rather the hurting woman won. Why was this such an effective statement? Because Jesus knew we all could relate.

The Pharisees, the disciples, the people gathered at the temple, the woman caught in the act, the person reading this book right now, and me, the author, all know how it feels to be caught, to sin, to fail, to be guilty, and to need mercy. That, my friend, is where healing language comes in.

They crowd began to leave. They walked away, realizing they had witnessed a miracle. This miracle was different, though. This miracle was not Jesus walking on water, feeding the multitudes, touching blind eyes and making them see, or even raising someone from the dead. This miracle was something new to this world.

This miracle was a miracle that introduced healing language. Where there was judgment, there was now mercy. Where there was condemnation, there was now consolation. Where there was guilt, there was now grace. Where there was much hurt, there was now healing. Where there was shame, there was now encouragement. Where there was even hate, there was now the power and presence of love.

While some saw the sin, Jesus saw the sinner. Don't get me wrong. Jesus does not condone this behavior. Oftentimes He was said to be nonjudgmental, and that is not true! Jesus did tell her to go and sin no more. He never condoned her behavior, but because of healing language, He condoned her potential. Wow!

What a story! What love! What healing! Jesus masterfully teaches all of us that healing language is a language all need to hear, use, and understand. Maybe He wasn't popular that day with the Pharisees. Maybe His own disciples questioned His motives. Maybe the crowd of people was perplexed, having never seen such healing language, but they all left knowing one thing for sure: Jesus cared. The passage closes so beautifully.

> *When Jesus had lifted up himself, and saw none but the woman, he said unto her, Woman, where are those thine accusers? hath no man condemned thee? She said, No man, Lord. And Jesus said unto her, Neither do I condemn thee: go, and sin no more* (John 8:10–11).

He got back up. Nobody was around. He waited until all were gone and asked the woman where her accusers were. He asked if any had condemned her. She said, "No man, Lord." Then Jesus, who was the only one there without sin, forgave her. He spoke healing language in his actions, in his stand, and with His words. He made sure she knew that she was forgiven.

Jesus was and still is today always more interested in where someone is going rather than where they have been. Don't get me wrong—with sin comes consequences. If we break the law, we have to pay for it. What happens in many cases, though, is society hangs onto the past and never lets go of it so much so that no proper healing ever takes place. Healing language is simply saying, "I know where you've been. I've been there too. I know your hurt. I have hurt too. I know you've fallen. I've fallen too. Let's get back up together and move on with life!"

When I was a little boy, my father said to me, "You did wrong, you had to be punished, but I still believe in you." I experienced healing language that night and many other times as well. I've been in ministry for twenty-five years, most of those years as a senior pastor, and I've made many mistakes in my dealings with people. I strive to use healing language now more than ever.

We would never harass a broken leg trying to heal. We would keep a severe cut clean that may have required stitches so it can properly heal. We would take the necessary prescribed medication to recover from a sinus infection or bronchitis. Unfortunately, all over the world we continue to pour salt in the wounds of many emotions by the words we say and actions we take.

Healing language realizes and understands that the spirit and mind can be wounded just as much, if not more so than a leg or an eye. The emotions and psychology of an individual who has been greatly wounded by the wrong words can also begin to heal with the right words. The important observation to make regarding this passage we just unpacked about Jesus and this woman caught in sin is that it wasn't just the words that Jesus said or didn't say that brought healing, it was the actions as well. The long pause, the presumed eye contact, the possible smile, the writing on the ground, and the patience were all a part of healing language.

Our world is full of hurting people. Just observe how many parents speak to their children in public places. Observe how politicians speak to each other and about each other. Bullying in schools is a serious problem. Churches are full of wounded spirits and hurting individuals. The hurt is real and the hurt is rampant, and in almost all cases medication won't help heal these issues. Words—the power of healing language. Smiles—the power of healing language.

We could go on and on. As we close this chapter, the good news is that you and I can become students of healing language.

A merry heart doeth good like a medicine: but a broken spirit drieth the bones (Proverbs 17:22).

What a verse! When we live out healing language in our daily actions, we can't help but have a merry heart. It will do us good like a medicine. We can be a part of a revival that starts right here, right now, with all of us helping heal broken spirits and dried-up bones.

This world needs some healing language now more than ever! As a little boy I witnessed it and remember the event like it was yesterday. The woman caught in the act of adultery, as well as thousands of others in her day, saw firsthand a Man living out healing language that transformed lives. Healing language is still transforming lives today.

If you are hurting today, find somebody you know who uses healing language. If you know someone today who is hurting, go out and demonstrate the power of healing language. Remember, what someone did does not equate to what that someone may do, and you and I might just make the difference. Let's live healing language. We might change some lives and salvage our fellow Christian brothers and sisters.

Four

Where the Heart Should Be

Thy wife shall be as a fruitful vine by the sides of thine house: thy children like olive plants round about thy table (Psalm 128:3).

When Jesus therefore saw his mother, and the disciple standing by, whom he loved, he saith unto his mother, Woman, behold thy son! Then saith he to the disciple, Behold thy mother! And from that hour that disciple took her unto his own home (John 19:26–27).

Growing up as I did with deaf parents, a deaf sister, deaf grandparents, and engulfed in the deaf world meant a much different upbringing for me. The dominant language of my life was American Sign Language.

Don't get me wrong, I obviously spoke English at school and when hanging out with friends or neighborhood kids. Home, though, was quite special. The dinner conversations were made by hands and facial expressions in between bites of our meals and sips of our drinks. The laughter or the serious conversations were measured differently than when I sat at a dinner table with many of my peers and contemporaries.

Having said all of this, I want to give you a sample conversation my brother, my sister, or I had with school friends growing up.

"Randy," called out my friend.

"Yo!" I said. We said yo a lot in the 1980s.

"Want to hang out this weekend?"

"Sure! I'd love to!"

"Can I come over to your house?"

"Sure! Why can't I come over to yours?"

"Well, Randy, I'd rather come over to yours."

"Why?" I asked.

"No reason. I just want to."

"OK! Sounds good! See you Saturday morning!"

For years I wondered why when my friends and I got together, 90% of the time it was at my house. You can ask the same of my brother Nick (hearing) and my sister Jennifer (deaf). We always had friends over. They would come over and hang out. We'd play ball, and we'd play Nintendo, old school Nintendo. Tecmo Bowl and Super Tecmo Bowl were some of our favorites. As time passed, I asked different friends why they loved coming to my house growing up.

Sometimes I'd be so blunt to ask if they liked the fact that my parents were deaf and that they could "take advantage" of that, although there were many times I questioned my parents' deafness. You couldn't hide anything from them. I know. I tried! It must be that sixth sense they talk about. I wondered and wondered. Most of my friends growing up never made much of an attempt to learn sign language.

This was consistent all over the country. I knew because we moved a lot. I was born in Florida, and then we moved to Utah where my brother was born. California was next, followed by Texas where my sister was born. Oklahoma followed, then we moved back to Florida. Again, we moved to California and then spent the remainder of my high school years in Kentucky.

Then it was Pennsylvania, back to Kentucky, and then finally Missouri, where my parents have now lived for twenty-plus years. As I already mentioned, my father was a popular educator and a great example to deaf children all across the country, and so the many moves followed many opportunities. The same could be said of my mother, as she also taught and had some powerful influence on young deaf children all across the country.

So, I lived in Florida twice and California twice, and several places in between. In all of those moves I went through different ages, schools, cultures, regions, and neighborhood kids, but it didn't matter where it was, all of our friends, and I mean all of them, always wanted to be at our house for sleepovers and other activities and not their own. Why?

As I got older and then was born again and converted by Jesus, I started to realize what the reason was. My parents hardly communicated with most of my friends and the friends of my brother for obvious reasons. They were always cordial to each other, and my many friends learned basic sign language just to say hi and greet them, but nothing beyond that. So, they didn't communicate, but my friends loved my parents! Why? Because my deaf father and my deaf mother spoke home language. Home language! What is that? I'm glad you asked.

There is no doubt that our homes are under great attack in America today and even globally. The breakdown of the home is so real, and we are seeing the drastic impact of that on our society daily. Schools are suffering because of this, churches suffer as well, and many neighborhoods have gone from being safe to dangerous all over our country because of the breakdown of our homes.

Home language? What is it? It's the product of an individual who speaks Heart Language regularly. It finally dawned on me as I got older that the reason many of my friends loved being at the Dignan home so much was because they felt at home. They were welcomed by two deaf adults who could not even communicate with them via regular conversation, but they communicated with welcoming spirits, kind facial expressions, and even funny gestures.

I did interpret many conversations between my parents and my friends, but it was the atmosphere of our home that was so welcoming. We lived in so many different homes— some were nice, some average, and some quite nice. The houses didn't welcome my friends; the home did.

A house is just a structure. It's drywall, nails, screws, insulation, trusses, brick, siding, plumbing, and electricity, but a home is heart, smiles, love, laughter, peace, joy, mercy, and forgiveness. America, and the rest of the world as well, has many houses but not as many homes.

My father and mother did not necessarily raise us in a Christian home. We were often churchgoers, but how many churches do you know that try to cater to the deaf? We were a moral family with old-fashioned discipline and respect for authority, but my parents knew Heart Language, which paved the way for home language. That was the difference!

When you sat at the Dignan table growing up, you felt welcome even though you couldn't sign; you felt loved even though you couldn't call my parents Dad or Mom, and you

37

felt as though you were family even though no DNA test would prove that you were. My father and my mother, for lack of a better term, spoke home language!

Thy wife shall be as a fruitful vine by the sides of thine house: thy children like olive plants round about thy table (Psalm 128:3).

This verse is a beautiful picture of unity. The fruitful vine and the table are mentioned. The home is so sacred and so special to God that He speaks of it highly in the Bible. The home needs unity, but that unity stems from stability, love, peace, guidance, and understanding. A home should never be measured by education, how many cars are in the garage, how many televisions mount the walls, or the value of the house in dollars.

A home is measured by the spirit, the peace, and the love that hold it all together. We would never want to live in a straw house. We know what happened to that little pig. We would never want to build a house that would blow over after the first thunderstorm, yet we constantly allow our homes to be weak, leading to collapse and ruin. There is hope, though—home language—and it is readily available to any and all. Let's look at Jesus and what He says about home language.

When Jesus therefore saw his mother, and the disciple standing by, whom he loved, he saith unto his mother, Woman, behold thy son! Then saith he to the disciple, Behold thy mother! And from that hour that disciple took her unto his own home (John 19:26–27).

Did He really just say that? He is hanging on the cross. He is about to die. He has suffered like no man has ever suffered so that you and I can be free from our sin, guilt, and shame. He is hurting physically, emotionally, spiritually, and psychologically.

He looks up, He looks around, and then He looks down, and there she is—Mom. She is the one who brought Him into this world, the one who loved Him, and the one who highly recommended Him for His miracle working ways in John 2. There she is, no doubt grieving at the sight of the Messiah, the Son of God, the Savior of our souls, and her son. He looks at her and His beloved disciple John, and because of the track record that was there and their years of ministry together, Jesus makes sure His mother is cared for.

While dying unselfishly, He still thinks of others. He helps the thief on the cross. He utters powerful sayings that we still meditate on to this day. He lies in the balance between eternity and earth. He is sacrificially giving Himself for all mankind. He is reflecting on His impact on this planet. He is waging war against the spiritual wickedness of this universe. Then, there is Mom.

Yes, Jesus had a mom, and Jesus loved her as she loved Him. Jesus, the master of Heart Language, the administrator of helpful language, the giver of healing language, takes care of Mom (flesh and blood) and John (not flesh and blood) because of home language. Home language is not defined by chromosomes, DNA, or blood, but rather love, unity, compassion, understanding, and forgiveness. Wow! This world desperately needs home language.

As a pastor I reflect on the many times I heard a man, woman, or teenager say, "Pastor, the church family is more my family than my own flesh and blood." As a pastor, that is a statement I have mixed emotions about. I am glad that the church may have helped fill a void, but the struggle is that the void shouldn't be there.

As you read this right now, realize that you are a son, a daughter, a husband, a wife, a father, a mother, a brother, a sister, a grandfather, a grandmother, an uncle, an aunt, a cousin, or even a step-parent. The titles are given by birth and last-name assignments. However, that is just the start. Let's go to the next level and learn from Jesus, Arthur Dignan, and Joyce Dignan how to speak, use, and communicate with home language. Do you know why we will all get along in heaven forever and ever? Because heaven's language is home language!

You can use home language at work, at church, in public, and most definitely at home. We have the opportunity right now to make the most of our homes and our families. We can go home tonight. Don't just go to your house; go to your home.

Realize there are children who call you Dad and Mom who need you, and there are parents who love you, and there are empty "tables" of unity (Psalm 128:3) all over this world waiting to be sat at. Let's pull up a chair this very evening, gather the family all around, and say, "Welcome to our Home!"

"Randy!"

"Yeah!"

"Want to hang out this weekend?"

"Sure! Sounds good! Want to meet up at the mall or at your house? I can ride my bike over!"

"No . . . uh . . . if it's OK with your parents, can I come over to your house?"

"Sure! I mean, I'll ask, but I am sure it is OK."

"Cool, Randy! I'll see you then."

"Sounds good. See you Saturday!"

Thank you, Dad. Thank you, Mom. Thank You, Jesus.

Home language! Let's speak it; let's use it; let's live it. When you change the home, you can then change the world.

Five

Truly the Best Policy

And ye shall know the truth, and the truth shall make you free (John 8:32).

One of the neat things about growing up with deaf parents, especially deaf educators, was the opportunity on many occasions to attend functions at the deaf schools where they worked. I have already touched on this briefly, but it is important to note that almost every state in the United States of America has what we call residential deaf schools. Some states have more than one.

These schools were established by the state governments and are funded by the taxes of the citizens of their respective states with a mission to educate children with hearing loss. For many of these children, their local communities and home towns were located hours away from their schools so they were not able to commute home daily. They lived in residential dormitories all school year long.

This practice continues today just about everywhere. There are even schools for children with hearing loss in other countries as well. In this modern era with good roads and better transportation, many of these children are able to commute to their homes and families each weekend throughout the school year. When my parents were growing up, they lived on campus at their respective schools of the Florida School for the Deaf and Blind in St. Augustine, Florida (my father), and the Ohio School for the Deaf in Columbus, Ohio (my mother), all year long.

The only exceptions would be to go home for Christmas and perhaps for Thanksgiving and spring break. I want to shed light on this fact because many people have no idea this was and still is a way of life for many people with hearing loss all across the country. Imagine, as a parent, that you would drop your kid off every Monday of the school year and not see them again until Friday. This includes children as young as kindergarten and first grade.

My parents often expressed to me how difficult this living and schooling situation was for them growing up—especially because my parents each had deaf parents, so going home for them was not a big deal. It was exciting. The majority of deaf children are born into homes with hearing parents, and unfortunately many of these parents don't make any attempt to learn sign language, making communication between parent and child sparse. I know many of these parents loved their child and cared for them, but none of them ever imagined having a deaf child, so communication from day one was complicated.

Today, we see a great wave of information being disseminated to these young, bewildered parents, and more resources are now available to help them navigate the early struggles of having a deaf child. My parents and my sister all had a head start because they were born into homes with deaf parents, so the struggles were greatly minimalized. (By the way, going back to our home language chapter, many of my deaf sister's friends loved coming to our house too because they could communicate with my parents more than they could their own.)

Because of this residential school issue, my father and mother spent many extra hours at the schools where they worked in and taught. Most educators teach all day, may lead up some clubs or even coach, but are able to disconnect from school because their students eventually go home for the evening. (By the way, if you are an educator of any sort and you are reading this book right now, I salute you and say thank you from the depths of my heart. You sir, and you ma'am, are true American heroes.)

My father and mother coached, ran extra clubs, hosted camps, tutored, and just spent time with the students. They literally became parents to them as they developed into adolescence and even early adulthood. My father and mother had close loving relationships through the years with these many residential students.

I am going to brag a little here. My father and mother were almost always the most popular teachers on campus. My deaf sister would follow in their footsteps until she stopped teaching due to having her own children. She also was a student favorite. As you can see, I am very proud of and thankful for my deaf family members.

When my father's career was in full swing, he became a key leader in the deaf movement, in the different deaf communities, and in the schools nearby. He was in high demand to teach, lead, and coach the deaf students with whom he was working. He taught different subjects, was dean of men in some schools, specialized in some areas of teaching, and would eventually become a professor at more than one state university, teaching American Sign Language and Deaf Culture for the university's ITP (Interpreter Training Program).

While he was growing and expanding his career as an educator, he was approached by some leadership professionals to enter the LTP (Leadership Training Program) of his day. This program would train him to leave the walls of a classroom and launch out and become a principal or even a superintendent of the schools where he worked. I remember as a little boy seeing my father and mother hash out the pros and cons of this additional undertaking.

In the short term, more schooling and training would be necessary, but in the longer term, added responsibilities would demand more of his time. While my parents were discussing the options, my father decided to visit one of his deaf mentors who was a little older and had some experience in this area. He was a pretty well-known name in the deaf world, so he will remain nameless. My father approached him and asked him about this opportunity. The meeting was short. My father's decision was made up after this brief meeting. He would not pursue the LTP, and he would not ever become a principal or a superintendent. Why, you ask?

The answer my father received in no way implies that every superintendent or principal falls into this group described to my father by his mentor. I want that made clear. The answer given to him that changed my father's mind and closed the door on his pursuit of advanced leadership in the schools was simply this: My father's mentor told him that he was simply too honest a man to become a leader of that stature. What? Did we hear that right?

Yes, my father was told that he was too honest to take on a more administrative role. Again, I am not implying that this applies to all administrators, and on that note I am grateful for many of them who daily make a difference in the lives of our children all across the country. I am merely stating to you what my father's mentor told him. I have known my father for forty-four years, and I can testify that my father is an honest man. Dad, thank you!

The word "honest" is defined simply as honorable in principles, intentions, and actions; upright and fair; truthful and credible. I think we can all agree for the most part with the statement, "Nobody likes to be lied to." It doesn't matter if it is a family member, a coworker, a boss, a neighbor, a politician, or even a friend; we do not want to be lied to.

Honesty is still the best policy; however, it appears to have become a lonely policy in these days. Not many adhere to honesty and the principles of honesty that should govern our lives. Our world has become a world of lies, and we are seeing the consequences of living lies today.

Oh for somebody to just tell the truth, and better still, to live the truth. We live in an interesting time when lies have become more believable than truth. As I have heard stated, "Truth can be stranger than fiction." However, truth is always truth, no matter what. Winston Churchill said, "A lie gets halfway around the world before the truth has a chance to get its pants on." How true! I love this quote and try to live by it. "The truth apologizes to no man."

This is the reason for our verse at the start of the chapter.

And ye shall know the truth, and the truth shall make you free (John 8:32).

The truth alone does not set you free, but the knowledge of it does. When you live a life guided by the principles of Heart Language, honest language will automatically follow suit. Our countries need men, women, teenagers, and children who will live truth and speak truth. Honest people of integrity and character give an ailing society the exact antidote it needs to get well and survive. Jesus said it like this:

Jesus saith unto him, I am the way, the truth, and the life: no man cometh unto the Father, but by me (John 14:6).

Jesus didn't just speak truth, teach truth, and live truth; He was truth! Truth is something we take for granted. For example, if I have a toothache and I go see my dentist, you better believe I want a dentist who is honest and tells the truth. If I am ill, I desire the same of a doctor. I want a doctor who will be honest and tell me the truth.

We live in a day and age where we only respond to what we want to hear and not the truth. The truth has become offensive, harsh, and even rejected. However, the truth is so important; when we live by Heart Language, we can't help but use honest language as well.

Jesus was truthful about the state of man. He was truthful about sin, eternal matters, and the struggles we all face and have. He was honest about the home, relationships, and about our relationship with God. He was honest about His disciples and their lack of faith.

He is still honest about my own lack of faith. On that note, He is also honest about heaven, joy, grace, and mercy. He is honest about love. I could go on and on. The truth is what we always need to hear. We need honest fathers, honest mothers, honest husbands, honest wives, honest politicians, honest bosses, honest pastors—the list is endless. Heart Language compels honest language. Honest language is a powerful by-product of Heart Language.

Jesus had a ministry that was 100% honest. He ruffled a lot of feathers and rubbed many people wrong, but He always told the truth. He always taught the truth. He couldn't help Himself because He spoke with Heart Language. A parent speaks honest language to his/her toddler when he/she is playing near the street because of Heart Language.

Honest language can save lives, heal hurting people, lead fallen people out of the ditches of life, and restore relationships. The truth is, we don't like to hear that we have a cavity, but we sure are grateful when it is fixed. We don't like when the doctor tells us our cholesterol is high and we need to lose weight, but after we implement the hard work and eat better for a while, we are thankful. It works!

Honest language can do the same for us spiritually. Honest language can heal our souls and comfort our minds. That is why Christians need a steady diet of God's Word. Daily we eat for physical nourishment and strength, and the same applies spiritually. We need daily doses of honesty from God that will nourish us and help us gain the strength we need to live out Heart Language.

"Well, Art Dignan, to be frank with you, you wouldn't make a good administrator. You are too honest."

Thank you, Dad, for being honest and for speaking honest language.

Six

To Go High, Go Low

Whosoever therefore shall humble himself as this little child, the same is greatest in the kingdom of heaven. And whoso shall receive one such little child in my name receiveth me (Matthew 18:4–5).

In the last chapter I spent some time bragging on the character of my deaf father and his determination to live by honest language. This chapter I am going to shift the focus to my mother. She has been an amazing example to hundreds and hundreds of young deaf children. Before we get into the main purpose for this chapter, I want to take some time to give you some statistics about children born with hearing loss. Here is some information about deaf children and the sources of this information.

General Statistics Regarding Deafness

• An estimated 1 in 1,000 babies is born deaf.

• Deafness is the number one birth defect in the U.S.

• 12 out of every 1,000 persons under the age of 18 is deaf. [NCHS]

- 30 out of every 1,000 children have hearing loss. [HLAA]
- 20% of individuals in the U.S. have some form of hearing loss. [HLAA]
- Approximately 4,000 new cases of sudden deafness occur each year in the United States. [Deafandhoh.com]
- More than 400 forms of hereditary deafness have been identified.
- Between 20% and 40% of individuals with an unknown source of hearing loss are deafened by the Connexin 26 gene.
- More than 50% of deafness in children is hereditary deafness. [NIH/Gallaudet Stat]
- 360 million people worldwide have a disabling hearing loss (a loss over 40 dB). [WHO]
- 3%–6% of deaf children have Usher syndrome. [Deafnadhoh.com]
- Only 4% of deaf children attend college. [UNC]

These statistics are eye opening and thought provoking. To add to this, my father traveled the country speaking at many workshops introducing what he researched to be the 90/10 theory. This theory was based on research my father did while he was working as a professor and teaching deaf culture to aspiring sign language interpreters.

This information was uncovered in the early 1990s. My father spent the bulk of his career educating deaf children and deaf adolescents, and the latter part of his career educating hearing people about deaf culture and the deaf world. The 90/10 theory introduces some interesting concepts.

Following are the approximate results based on my father's research:

- 90% of deaf children are born to hearing parents.
- 10% of deaf children are born to deaf parents.
- 90% of deaf children graduate high school at a fourth-grade reading level or lower.
- 10% of deaf children graduate high school with a higher reading level than fourth grade.
- 90% of deaf children start school behind the average hearing child academically.
- 10% of deaf children start school on track in comparison to their hearing contemporaries.

Are we starting to see a trend? I grew up seeing the truth of these statistics on a regular basis, and this trend has continued into the new century. You might wonder how this is possible.

Let's set up the scenario. A couple has been married for some time. Things are going along great. They just bought a new home. Their lives are blessed. They decide to have a child. The doctor acknowledges that they are expecting a child, and they are so excited and share the good news with their family, their friends, their church family, and maybe even their neighbors.

The nursery at home is decorated, and their anticipation grows. The day finally arrives, and their precious baby is born. After spending a few days in the hospital, they head home and bring their new bundle of joy with them.

Time passes, and they notice that the baby doesn't seem

to be responding to loud noises. They begin to feel alarmed. The baby seems completely normal in every other area of growth and development. The doctor runs some tests, and the tests come back positive that their precious baby has severe hearing loss. The official diagnosis is that the child is deaf.

At this point I recall to your attention the aforementioned statistic that approximately 90% of deaf children are born to hearing parents. From 2000 and beyond, these diagnoses haven't been too devastating to many hearing parents because of advancements in technology and because of more general awareness and information regarding the deaf world and deaf culture.

Before 2000, though, many parents would have left that doctor's office devastated. They would have asked questions like: "What will we do? How will we ever communicate with our child? How will our child learn to read and write? How will they get along in society?" These questions have been asked many times through the years.

Compare and contrast that story to this one. My sister, Jennifer Morales, in 2016 gave birth to my beautiful niece Amelia. Jennifer and her husband Jorge are both deaf. Amelia was born in April 2016. I remember my wife and I visiting our new niece in the hospital. We were so excited to meet her.

As a pastor, I have visited hundreds of newborn babies in hospitals, and almost all of them were born hearing and everything was just fine. I also noticed that almost every newborn spends most of their first few days sleeping—a lot! Our niece did not sleep like many babies born in the same hospital that day. Why?

Because she had not had the same previous noise stimulation and exposure in the womb as all other hearing babies. Those babies heard their parents' voices, maybe even the voices of older siblings, and even the television and music during their gestation. My niece, as is the case with most babies born deaf, experienced true stimulation upon birth. Light is perhaps the biggest stimulus.

My wife and I remember our little niece constantly staring at the lights of the hospital room. She was not going to sleep at all. She seemed amazed to see this bright stimulation we call light on her first day of birth.

Several weeks passed, and I was invited to be with my sister as Amelia was having her hearing tested. I overheard the nurse say to someone, "The poor little girl is deaf." My sister was in another room, and I immediately relayed that information to her. She smiled and shook her head, expecting that to be the response. The nurse walked into the room with an uneasy expression.

I immediately looked at her and said, "Ma'am, it's OK, you can tell her."

The nurse asked, "Are you sure?"

I replied, "Yes."

She looked at my sister and said, "Your daughter's hearing tests have come back positive that she has severe hearing loss. I am sorry."

I immediately conveyed my sister's response. She said, "It is OK. We will be just fine!"

And four years later, they are just fine. My niece is signing fluently, learning all she can soak up, and getting greatly spoiled by her favorite uncle. That's right, Nick! I am her favorite.

Why, you may ask, am I sharing all of this with you? Because it is important to understand that most people have never even met a deaf person in their lives; and if they did, it was a brief meeting due to the lack of communication.

Remember what we said earlier in this book that people often fear what they don't know. Many well-meaning people are simply ignorant of this amazing, yet unnoticed culture of people who belong to the deaf world. One of the three main purposes of this book is to put forth some knowledge about this incredible people group. I write this book also to honor my parents and my deaf heritage, to inform the millions of readers I expect to read this book, and to share life-changing application from the life of Jesus and Heart Language.

Enter my mother again. Early in my life I noted my mother taking an extra interest in the younger deaf children of the residential deaf schools in which both of my parents worked. My mother had almost a burden for them. She knew the many stories of her peers and contemporaries growing up who said they would rather live at school than at home with their own flesh and blood.

She recalled the many stories her friends and classmates relayed to her of horrible Thanksgiving and Christmas experiences being the only deaf person around all other hearing family members, of attending church services with all of their hearing family members and getting nothing out of the services because there were no sign language interpreters. My mother remembers being able to read much better than her peers. She remembers entering school with young boys and girls her age who were developmentally two to three years behind her in basic education and knowledge.

Why is this? Remember my father's 90/10 theory? I am

in no way trying to point fingers or blame the parents of these deaf children, or even the professionals like doctors, audiologists, or even teachers for the many deaf children who were behind the eight ball when they started school. Quite frankly, many of these parents and even professionals didn't know what would work or what was best for these precious deaf children.

In most cases, when you meet a deaf person, they will tell you, if asked, that they are the only deaf person in their family. That explains why they love to be around their "own." The deaf schools provide them a haven, a community, a place of acceptance where they can thrive, develop, and grow.

It is noted that the deaf culture is the only worldwide culture with no native homeland. This makes perfect sense because every culture within itself has deaf people. Russia has deaf born in their country regularly, as does China, the Bahamas, and of course the United States of America.

For example, a hearing child is born in Mexico and is immediately exposed to language, Spanish, culture, the Latino way, learning, voices of parents and older siblings, and even peers their age. From day one they just fit right in! The deaf child born in Mexico has a 90% chance of having all hearing family members. They start out behind from the beginning because they miss out on language—the hearing of sounds and voices. I am in no way trying to garner sympathy for the deaf population. I just feel the real need to educate and inform our society about one of this world's most amazing people groups—the deaf.

My mother spent many extra hours with deaf children, working with them on reading, comprehension, and communication development. These children are not unintelligent;

they are not even learning disabled. They simply need custom designed teaching methods that cooperate with their native sign languages in their respective cultures. These children need to learn their native language before they can learn their spoken and written languages.

My parents and sister from the very start were exposed to American Sign Language, and it was their foundational language so that they could more easily learn English. Much of this world knows multiple languages, but in order to learn the "next" language, you must have a native foundational language to start. For the deaf in America, it is American Sign Language. Once they begin to grasp ASL, they can then begin to learn English.

My mother recognized and understood that most of the deaf children she was working with just needed some extra encouragement and mentorship so that they might grow and develop in their education. To work with any child takes patience, consistency, and most of all, love. I watched my mother love hundreds of deaf children and watched her teach them to read and write. She prepared them for advanced elementary grades, middle school, and then of course, high school.

I have seen dozens and dozens of deaf students graduate high school through the years and have seen them thank my mother personally, and even sometimes publicly, because of her investment in them. My mother loved these deaf children as if they were her own. She labored with them, she caught their tears of frustration, and she encouraged them. Even to this day, at the time of the writing of this book, she is teaching her own granddaughter as well as a few other deaf children basic education in a preschool setting.

Whosoever therefore shall humble himself as this little child, the same is greatest in the kingdom of heaven. And whoso shall receive one such little child in my name receiveth me (Matthew 18:4–5).

It takes a level of humility to work with a child. Some of our choicest servants in society today are the fine educators of our youth. My brother Nick (hearing) and my sister Jennifer (deaf) took after our mother. They also are very skilled and patient when it comes to working with the very young. My father and I, not so much! I love teenagers and speak to ten to fifteen thousand of them every year, but primary-age kids, well, that's a different story.

Jesus Himself says, "We are to be humble like the little child. We are to receive them." These are powerful and profound truths shared by Jesus. He was a master at connecting with every age group, race, background, and culture because of His Heart Language. With Heart Language comes the ability to exercise humble language, which brings you down to the level of a child. I love this quote: "No man stands so tall as when he stoops to help a child." Wow! What a truth. One chapter later we see . . .

Then were there brought unto him little children, that he should put his hands on them, and pray: and the disciples rebuked them. But Jesus said, Suffer little children, and forbid them not, to come unto me: for of such is the kingdom of heaven. And he laid his hands on them, and departed thence (Matthew 19:13–15).

I love this story. Jesus showed a level of humility. As Jesus' disciples hurried the children away from Him, Jesus called for them to come unto Him. He spent some time with them and paid attention to them. So many times in life we find our busy minds not paying attention to the youngest ones. Sadly, many of those younger minds call us Dad and Mom, yet we don't quite give them the attention they really need.

It is vital that I follow the example of my mother, and even more so Jesus, and humble myself and invest in the next generation. These children want to be taught, they want to grow and develop, and most of all they want to be loved.

I shall never forget a day in my life several years ago when I learned a valuable lesson about children. I was driving our church bus as we were taking teenagers to pass out flyers for an upcoming event at our church. I had dropped off half of the teens on one side of a neighborhood and the other half on the other side. I then decided to park in the middle and wait for them to meet me there.

As I was sitting on the bus working on my phone, I heard a knock on the bus door. I looked down and saw a young boy. I opened the door, and what happened next will be something I will never forget the rest of my life.

"Hi there," said the boy. "What are you doing?"

"I am sitting on this bus waiting for our teenagers. They are passing out flyers for an exciting event we have at our church. In fact, how old are you? You might be able to come."

"I am four!"

Well, he was a bit young for this event, but surely I could make an exception.

"Wow! Great! Well, maybe you can come. Here is a flyer you can take back home to your parents."

The little boy looked down at the ground and sheepishly said, "My parents don't live with me. My mom is gone, and my dad is in jail."

My heart ached. Another victim of the breakdown of the

home. Our country won't be fixed by a Republican or a Democrat or a president or a governor. Our country can get the help it needs and begin to heal again if our homes would get strong again and follow the pattern laid out for us in the Bible.

"I'm sorry, buddy. Here is a flyer anyway. We would love to have you!"

"Thank you!" the boy said. "Can I ask you one more question?"

"Sure!" I said.

"Can I have a hug? I don't get very many hugs."

What? I was a complete stranger. I had just pulled up to park my bus. This boy did not know anything about me. What did I do? It is a very strange day and age in which we live, and unfortunately church leaders have to take extra precautions to protect themselves. What did I do?

"Sure!" I said.

The boy bounced right up the stairs and jumped onto my lap and gave me a big hug. I hugged him back. He jumped off my lap with the flyer in hand and walked away with a big smile on his face. I sat there for a while just stunned. Tears were rolling down my cheeks.

I was—ready for this—humbled. Another five minutes later, our teens started to load the bus. For those five minutes I just thought about what a difference we could all make if we would just love the little children. I think there is a song about that. I wondered how many times I missed out on being a blessing to a little child because I wasn't humble enough.

As I continue to embrace Heart Language living, I find myself more willing to exercise humble language as well! Humble language—the language that can change the world, one child at a time. Thank you, Mom. Thank You, Jesus.

Seven

Don't Worry; Just Be

There is a lad here, which hath five barley loaves, and two small fishes: but what are they among so many? And Jesus said, Make the men sit down. Now there was much grass in the place. So the men sat down, in number about five thousand. And Jesus took the loaves; and when he had given thanks, he distributed to the disciples, and the disciples to them that were set down; and likewise of the fishes as much as they would. When they were filled, he said unto his disciples, Gather up the fragments that remain, that nothing be lost. Therefore they gathered them together, and filled twelve baskets with the fragments of the five barley loaves, which remained over and above unto them that had eaten (John 6:9–13).

Everybody in life wants to be happy. Happiness is something that is not a respecter of persons. A young child wants to feel happy just like the middle-age person does and the senior citizen does as well. In order to better understand where this particular language, happy language, is going, let's be reminded of the definition of happy.

Happy is simply defined as delighted, pleased, glad, or favored by fortune. More and more people struggle finding happiness. They use the exact phrase, "I can't find happiness." It's as if mankind has been on a search to find happiness. Happiness can appear to be a lost treasure. Happiness is sometimes considered unattainable by some in society.

You also have to deal with the multiple different concepts of what constitutes true happiness. Is it money? Fame? A successful career? A successful marriage? A successful home? Retirement? A good education? A nice house? A vacation home? Or is it simply a state of well-being? Is it feeling good all of the time? Is it good health? Is it good fitness? Is it warm weather? Is it cold weather?

It's hard to define because we all know people who are happy who have money and others who are just as happy who don't have money. We also know people who are miserable who have money, and those who are miserable who don't have money. So, to better understand happiness, let's look at what God says about this subject.

God truly focuses on joy. Jesus speaks of joy in the Bible, and here is what He says about it.

And ye now therefore have sorrow: but I will see you again, and your heart shall rejoice, and your joy no man taketh from you (John 16:22).

God emphasizes joy. Why? Joy is a condition, while happiness is an emotion. Both are given to us by God. I think there is an error that teaches Christians should never be sad. God actually gave us all of these amazing emotions. Happiness, sadness, anger, laughter, and tears are all gifts from God and are to be experienced regularly throughout our lives.

The key is learning how to control our emotions rather than to be controlled by them. That is where joy comes in. Emotions can change from morning to afternoon. Joy is constant. For example, several times in my ministry, I visited a newborn baby in the hospital and then a few hours later preached a funeral. I was happy at the hospital with the parents and their newborn baby, but sad with the grieving family at the funeral home. But in both instances I had joy.

Joy is a condition. A Christian can experience joy in happy times and sad times. Emotions are affected by circumstances both internal and external. Joy is a condition that is internal but can affect the external.

So, what is true happiness? Heart Language is so powerful and helpful that when one lives by the principles of Heart Language, they can also tap into and live by the principles of happy language.

My brother Nick and I were successful football players in our younger years. We took after our father, who had a great football career at the Florida School for the Deaf and Blind and then later at Gallaudet University. Nick and I both won two state championships apiece during our junior and senior years of high school. We both earned nice large football rings that we still have to this day. In fact, we each gave one of our rings to our father who sat in the stadium and rooted for us every game.

My mother and sister also attended our games and were our biggest fans. An interesting thing happened to both my brother and me. I played my football in Kentucky, and after I graduated and went on to play college football, our family moved to Pennsylvania where my brother played his football and graduated there. In both locations, we were approached by our local newspapers to do a write-up on our family to talk about football and deaf culture.

How did they know? Well, interestingly enough, after every series during our football games, as my brother and I would leave the field or during a break in the action, we would try to find our father's face in the crowd of thousands, and he would coach us from the stands. Our coaches did not mind it, knowing our father's football pedigree, and they also knew our father watched us individually while the coaches watched the whole team.

Our father would sign to us from the stadium bleachers and instruct us. If he were hearing and tried to yell at us or talk to us, there would be no way we would ever hear him! Yet, because of sign language, he was able to communicate from the bleachers to the field of action. Sometimes he would sign "great play" or "great tackle" or "awesome sack." Other times he would sign, "You look lazy! Get after the ball."

He sent exhortations, rebukes, and suggested tips that helped us win our games. It was a very unique experience in that my brother and I both graduated with a football record 29 wins and 1 loss along with all-area honors, all-star selections, all-state selections, and multiple newspaper and radio interviews. We both were also heavily recruited to play division I football.

So, the local papers in Kentucky and Pennsylvania did write-ups about the football games and the effective way to communicate at these very loud games because of sign language. The story came across as happy and uplifting. This family with deaf and hearing members made the front page of our local newspapers in both states because of using sign language and communication at the weekly football games.

Fast-forward years later and to this subject of happy language, I have learned that when you win at anything, you can't help but be happy. Again, back to joy. I have won many times in life and been happy, and I have lost many times in life and been sad; but in both instances I had joy. So if we win, we have the potential to be happy. Whether it is a six-year-old boy winning his first football or basketball game, or an NFL player winning the Super Bowl, both young and old experience happiness individually and then as a team. Hence, the point of this chapter!

I find it logical that in these days of so much division, good people can't seem to find happiness. Depression is at an all-time high, and I am constantly counseling well-meaning individuals who simply want to be happy. I believe unity brings more potential for happiness.

Behold, how good and how pleasant it is for brethren to dwell together in unity! (Psalm 133:1).

Does this sound like a happy verse to you? It sure sounds that way to me. Let's look at our opening text again.

There is a lad here, which hath five barley loaves, and two small fishes: but what are they among so many? And Jesus said, Make the men sit down. Now there was much grass in the place. So the men sat down, in number about five thousand. And Jesus took the loaves; and when he had given thanks, he distributed to the disciples, and the disciples to them that were set down; and likewise of the fishes as much as they would. When they were filled, he said unto his disciples, Gather up the fragments that remain, that nothing be lost. Therefore they gathered them to-

gether, and filled twelve baskets with the fragments of the five barley loaves, which remained over and above unto them that had eaten (John 6:9–13).

Wow! What a story. A young lad, Jesus, disciples, five thousand men, plus women and children . . . This is amazing! How in the world are we going to get all of these people united? The potential for happiness will be off the charts if this crowd can be united. The people are hungry. The need is great.

A young lad volunteers his lunch. Jesus intervenes with His disciples, who are united and willing. A miracle happens. We see the genius of Jesus and Heart Language. Jesus, the original Creator and Teacher of Heart Language, is teaching His followers to exercise Heart Language. That Heart Language brings forth unity and the potential for happy language.

Imagine if every family united around Heart Language and lived it out. What if we worked together more rather than staying divided? What if our politicians could put aside their many petty divisions and unite for the greater good? What if CEOs, presidents, vice presidents, and managers could unite to make their company's work forces happier? What if dads and moms and the children could unite as family? What if churches, pastors, staff, and members of the body would unite around the "majors" and not be bothered with the "minors?"

What if? I ask, "Why not?" I still remember being a six-teen-year-old and then a seventeen-year-old and running off the field after winning the biggest game of the season and hugging my dad, my mom, my brother, my sister, as well as many other family members and friends. I did not win the state championship twice alone. I won with my team, and we were happy. I won with my family, and we were happy.

Jesus could literally have done whatever He wanted alone, by Himself. However, if you notice as you study the Gospels, you see Him including His disciples in the miracles and activities regularly to teach them that the more we work and strive together, the more we win together. There is so much unnecessary division in our world today.

Have we become so shallow that we divide over skin color, background differences, culture differences, and financial statuses? We need to unite more than ever so we can win more than ever. Teamwork makes the dream work. Benjamin Franklin said, "We must, indeed, all hang together or, most assuredly, we shall all hang separately." So true! This quote has the potential for happy language or unhappy language.

The very country I was born in, the United States of America, has sadly become the Divided States. We must work to change this! We must baptize this nation with Heart Language so the potential for happy language can be drastically improved.

Jesus wanted His disciples united to win together and to be happy together. We have to see how true and possible this is. My father signed to me while I was playing football on the field to make me better. He wanted me to win. I played, but we won together. We were happy together. This is so possible for everybody if Heart Language becomes a part of our lives.

Fast-forward years later, and I am now a pastor for almost twenty-five years. I travel and speak twenty-two to twenty-eight weeks out of the year at youth camps, youth conferences, deaf fellowships, and missions meetings, and my family is almost always present with me. They sing songs while I sign them (you do not want to hear me sing) for crowds of thousands, sometimes right before I get up to speak and preach. I love having our family serve together because we can also win together, which helps us be happy together.

Where could we look at each of our lives and see where we can improve on unity and capitalize on happy language? People so often feel alone out there. I often hear in my counseling sessions statements and questions like these:

"I feel so alone."
"I just want to be happy."
"How can I be happy again?"
"Why do I feel so lonely?"
"I feel like nobody understands me."
"Does anybody care?"
"What can I do to be happy again?"

These statements and questions can be answered with hope and the potential for happiness, if we would all just start living out Heart Language.

Jesus had one main mission, and we know that was to go to the cross and then out of the tomb. On His journey to the cross, however, He desired for His followers to learn that true happiness is in teamwork and putting others first. It is possible for anybody.

In other words, Jesus was most happy when He helped others become happy. Back to my football team. You have linemen, quarterbacks, running backs, receivers, defensive personnel, and all of them have different responsibilities, but when they help each other out, we all win. So what is happiness?

How do you define happiness? Happiness, ultimately, is a decision. You and I can decide right now to be happy. If you are reading this book right now and don't feel so happy, put the book down for a bit and talk to, call, or text somebody on your "team" of life, and say, "Let's form a team and let's be happy."

Husbands and wives, decide right now to be a team and win at the game of life. Heart Language is the decision, God is the coach, and happy language is the result of the decision to unite around Heart Language! Pastor friend, right now decide that you are going to have a happy church. Decide that this Sunday morning you are going to stand before the people God has given you to lead, and you will unite them with happy language. CEO of a company, president of a business, vice president of a start-up, decide right now that you and your team will unite and that happy language will be a regular occurrence in the workplace.

Many days when you are out in the field of life with your team, your family, your coworkers, your friends, and your church, you can look to the stands and know God is signaling to you in Heart Language, and with it, all on the field may experience happy language.

Let's unite around this decision and make unity and togetherness a priority in our lives. There are many lonely and sad people out there who want to be loved and to belong, and Heart Language can teach them happy language again. This applies to everybody and anybody. You can be happy again and experience happy language. Make the decision now, pray about it, ask Jesus for His help, and unite together to win.

Jesus mastered the ability to win in every situation. In the most bleak of situations, including the brutal crucifixion, Jesus knew that the mission was a go and He was united with

His Father; three days later, we all won. "He is risen!" That's what the Bible says. You see, Jesus experienced the lowest of lows a human could experience one day, then the highest of highs three days later.

No matter what we go through in life, whether low or high, Jesus knows about it. When we hit the lower points of life, Jesus knows the lowest; and when we hit the higher points of life, Jesus hit the highest. So, we can unite with Him and with loved ones, and because of Jesus and His labor of love, we can experience heart and happy language on a regular basis.

"Nick Dignan on the tackle once again," said the announcer. It was the fall of 1993. I was at the game. Big brother was watching. I had a college game the next day. My little brother was playing football. It was Friday night lights. I miss these games. I had graduated and was now playing college football.

I looked over at my father. His arms were waving through the air with passion and excitement. Oh yes, deaf people sign bigger when they are excited or, uh, even mad. I have been the recipient of those big signs many times in my life. Dad was fired up. His son just made a tackle! He is signing, "Good job, keep working, don't let up because we have to win this game."

We did. We won. The post-game fellowship and meal were awesome. Little did I know that my father and mother attended every game with Heart Language, and win or lose that night, we would all communicate with happy language. Happy language . . . it is for you and me to live and use. Let's do it. Life is too short. Love. Unite. Win. Be happy. Thank you, Dad! Thank you, Mom! Thank You, Jesus!

Eight

Not a Wishing Well

And a woman having an issue of blood twelve years, which had spent all her living upon physicians, neither could be healed of any, Came behind him, and touched the border of his garment: and immediately her issue of blood stanched. And Jesus said, Who touched me? When all denied, Peter and they that were with him said, Master, the multitude throng thee and press thee, and sayest thou, Who touched me? And Jesus said, Somebody hath touched me: for I perceive that virtue is gone out of me. And when the woman saw that she was not hid, she came trembling, and falling down before him, she declared unto him before all the people for what cause she had touched him, and how she was healed immediately. And he said unto her, Daughter, be of good comfort: thy faith hath made thee whole; go in peace (Luke 8:43–48).

Now that we have looked into the concept of happy language, it is time to look at hopeful language. By this point in the book, I sincerely hope we are trying to live out the principles of Heart Language as demonstrated by my parents and mostly by Jesus Himself. Hope is an important part of life in

70

these busy days, and it appears to be lacking. Many people feel hopeless.

They struggle finding hope in what they view as a hopeless world. Let's define the word hope and make sure there is clarity in understanding the presentation of this chapter. Hope simply means the feeling that what is wanted will turn out for the best. It also means to look forward to with desire and reasonable confidence.

The reason I picked the scriptural passage at the beginning of this chapter is because of the persistency of the woman "having an issue of blood twelve years." She would not give up. She had spent all her resources on physicians, and she had this illness for twelve years. She was sick and had nothing left. She was at a point many would call hopeless. Yet, she did not quit but held out hope. We'll get back to her in a minute.

My father and mother both grew up in educational settings not conducive to their needs. We have already addressed that in a previous chapter, so I would like us to go a different direction in this chapter. Hope is a doctrine of the Bible, and it is an attribute of Christians. The woman of Luke 8 and my parents will demonstrate how significant sharing hope can be.

And now abideth faith, hope, charity, these three; but the greatest of these is charity (1 Corinthians 13:13).

In Paul's famous "love" chapter to the church at Corinth, he mentions faith, charity (love), and hope. He says the greatest of these is charity, but hope "made the podium." Hope is a powerful attribute that human beings need to have on a regular basis. Jesus came to bring us hope. Children need hope. Couples need hope. The elderly need hope. We all need hope.

My parents became examples of hope to the next generation. We all know that we love to look back on some amazing historical experiences that worked out, to help us with the dilemmas of today. People who lived through hard circumstances of life with hope inspire many of us who look for hope in our current situations.

A coach losing a game may recall an amazing comeback from the past. A business owner about to lose everything remembers other famous businessmen in history who lost everything and yet flourished again. A parent with a wayward child looks to a friend or family member in their past who came around, and it gives them hope. A family who just got bad news about a loved one's health situation looks to other inspirational stories of healing for hope. A couple on the brink of divorce hears about another couple who was once where they are and are happily married now, and it gives them hope. A soldier on a distant battlefield, growing weary of his tour, remembers all the other soldiers who made it through, and it gives him hope. The aspiring doctor in med school, living on very little sleep, thinks of the thousands who have gone on before him and now practice, and it gives him hope. The patient recovering from total knee replacement surgery, feeling the pain, thinks of the friend who recovered from the same surgery and is up and walking well, and it gives him hope.

The purpose of this chapter and hope language is for us to become the givers of hope. We are beginning to regularly implement Heart Language in our daily lives and interactions, and with that comes helpful language, home language, happy language, and so on. We are discerning when to use Heart Language. We may use it at home, at our workplace, at church, or in kind daily interactions with complete strangers. Hopeful language is something we can give on a regular basis to the hopeless. I believe all of us have at one point in our lives felt hopeless, and we made it through. Now, we get to give others hope.

My parents struggled through their formative years of education. In fact, my father often says, "The deaf are not unintelligent or uneducated. Rather, they are miseducated." Again, we have already discussed this previously, but here's where it gets good. My parents can look every deaf child in the eye even today and simply say, "YOU CAN!" That, my friend, is giving hope.

We can all be the beneficiaries and givers of hope. It is a beautiful cycle. We experience hope; we receive hope; we give hope. Everybody has a story. Everybody's story can help somebody else in their story. There is somebody in your sphere of influence who needs you to give them hope.

My story is unique in that I grew up with deaf family members. I regularly meet young children who have deaf parents, and I immediately reach out to them and tell them how awesome it is to have deaf parents. Why? Because I know the difficulties, the misunderstandings, and society's ignorant view on the deaf world, and I want to give them encouragement and hope. The same can apply in so many areas of life.

Someone who has a particular illness can give the recently diagnosed person hope. God made our world interesting and diverse. I am so thankful for this, and I truly believe God wanted us to unite around our differences and learn from them. I have met deaf people from the Bahamas, Peru, the

Philippines, Ecuador, Jamaica, Russia, Japan, China, and many other places.

In those meetings I could not relate to the Chinese culture or the Japanese culture or the Russian culture. However, we were able to connect and bond around the deaf culture. The point is, I have many deaf black friends, and many deaf Mexican friends, and our connection to the deaf world bonds us even though our other cultures are different.

All in all, humans are more alike than we are different. Where we live, how we grew up, and which country we hail from all affect our lives and who we are, but we truly are more the same than we are different.

I have been pastoring over twenty years and been in the ministry almost twenty-five, and I have learned some things about mankind. We all cry, we all laugh, we all have the potential to love and want to be loved, we all forgive and want to be forgiven, and we all know what loneliness can be like.

God made all of us in amazing fashion. He knew that all of us would have many major differences, but He also knew we would all have major similarities. We bleed the same, and that blood is pumped through our veins by a beating heart. We all require sleep, some more than others; nevertheless, we all sleep. We all need and crave affection. We all thrive on hugs, eye contact, and gestures of love. We are aware of the joys of bringing a newborn into this world and the hurt of saying goodbye to a loved one who leaves this world.

We all have faced the uncertainties of life and struggled through our doubts and fears. We all have known what it feels like to get some great news one day, only to receive bad news a week later. It doesn't matter which continent we are from, and it doesn't matter that our cultures could be vastly different, we all have an innate desire to experience regular hope that says, "Hey! It's going to work out."

The world as a whole has lost hope because the focus of many societies concentrate more on what divides us rather than unites us. For example, in the United States of America, we see major schisms inside our political infrastructure that regularly bring out the worst in us. Democrats, Republicans, and Independents have all been guilty of unnecessary mud-slinging and negativity that weakens our bonds and divides us rather than unites us.

I do understand that there are times to separate and divide. I absolutely recognize the need to stand up for right and to take action regarding good over evil and right over wrong, but much of what we see today are unnecessary divisions that bring about pain and hurt, and not hope. Hope is to emotional pain what medicine is to physical pain. Hope dispels sadness on a regular basis and restores broken and ailing hearts.

We enter a world where, in many cases, the odds are stacked against us. Maybe someone is born in a third-world country. Maybe someone is born a different race and from day one grows up a minority. Maybe someone is born with a physical disability. Maybe someone is born into poverty. Maybe someone is born into a broken home. Maybe someone is born with an illness. Maybe someone is born into a bad situation. Or maybe, just maybe, you are born into a home and you are deaf and feel the odds are stacked against you. There is HOPE!

Our chapter's opening text tells of a woman who had an issue of blood in Luke 8:43–48. This woman was desperate for hope. The reason I love this passage so much is there is no question that Jesus exercises hope language here. Hope language takes Heart Language to a different level. Hope language is when one stops everything they are doing because one person, just one person, needs some help and reassurance.

Jesus was being followed by a crowd. People were bumping into Him, and the multitude thronged Him. When a woman touched the border of His garment, she was healed. Jesus asked who touched Him. He knew someone was needing hope. In our very busy schedules of today, we may need to look for hope seekers on purpose. They are everywhere.

We have this amazing opportunity to be like Jesus. We can appreciate and cherish the hope we have received and, in turn, be givers of hope. We can help dozens of people around us just by stopping and paying attention. Jesus paid attention to this woman and made her a priority. He said, "Somebody touched me." The phrase that follows, "I perceive that virtue has gone out of me," is an amazing statement. It literally means that I must stop what I am doing because somebody demands my attention right now.

This hopeless world is turning to alcohol, drugs, immorality, and even suicide because they feel no hope. The church has a Great Commission to bring hope to this world. While we may feel overwhelmed when we think about taking the Gospel to the whole world, Jesus, through Heart Language, teaches us that real change and hope come from the one-on-one relationships we pursue.

God pursued us. God loved us. God spends much of His work pursuing individuals. Yes, Jesus preached to the masses but think about the book of John again. John 3 showcases Jesus and Nicodemus, one-on-one. John 4 showcases Jesus and the woman at the well, one-on-one. John 5 showcases

Jesus and the man by the pool of Bethesda, one-on-one. John 6 showcases Jesus and the young lad with his lunch, one-on-one. John 8 showcases Jesus and the woman caught in the act of adultery, one-on-one. John 9 showcases Jesus and the blind man that gets healed, again one-on-one.

Jesus teaches us consistently that in order to reach the masses, we must make a difference one by one. So many are born into a world where, from day one, they are told that there is no hope and all the odds are stacked against them. You can't make it. You can't achieve anything. You will never experience success. All of these statements are lies. When we live with Heart Language as our main language, we become regular hope givers. We will have the awesome, exciting opportunity to give hope, share hope, talk hope, and live hope because we have also been the beneficiaries of hope.

Jesus Christ came to give hope. He gave hope to any and everybody. He did not hold back when somebody needed Him. He knew that many came to Him with preexisting conditions, stereotypes, rejections, and failures, but that they would leave with an abundance of hope that would change their lives.

Right now, there is someone you work with who desperately needs some hope. There is someone in your neighborhood who doesn't know if they are going to make it. There is someone that you bump into at your local store who feels doubts and fears on a regular basis. There is someone who sits near you at church that feels all alone and needs some hope. God wants us to be the one who looks them in the eye and gives them hope. God desires that we be like His Son Jesus who went out of His way to give someone hope.

There are so many ways we can do this. It starts with pursuing them. We can then ask questions and offer a listening ear. It is amazing how much people will open up when they feel like someone cares about them. This is something anybody can do. You do not need a college degree; you do not need a workshop; you just need to care.

Right now, put this book down and meditate on all of the blessed times you received hope. Maybe it was from a friend, a pastor, a family member, or maybe while you were reading your Bible when you were flooded with hope. Hope is a gift that is truly cyclical and will return to us over and over as we give out hope. I believe, in many cases, before people open up their hearts and give Jesus and the Gospel a chance, they desire evidence of the power of Christianity by measuring how much hope can be received. When the world sees the Christian living with hope, sharing hope, and believing hope, it becomes real to them as well.

The woman with the issue of blood heard about Jesus and had hope that if she could just get close to Him, she might get some hope. She got a whole lot more than just hope; she got healed and was made whole. Hope starts small but has the potential to grow strong. Maybe that's why 1 Corinthians 13 mentions hope along with faith and charity as three of the great things.

These three attributes can grow and grow and can benefit the one believing and practicing all three and then go beyond and benefit many others. Many start with a little bit of hope, seeking to grow their hope. The woman with the blood issue had just enough hope to get to Jesus, and Jesus took care of the rest. I wonder how many times the hopeless look to the Christian and wonder if they may get some hope from them only to be let down.

I have witnessed firsthand my father and my mother become almost like "rock stars" in the eyes of hundreds of young deaf children. The deaf observed my parents, as college graduates, driving their own cars, having a family, owning their own house, and loving life; and they found hope.

I have met many deaf adults through the years who asked me, "Are you Art Dignan's son?" Or, "Are you Joyce Dignan's son?" Of course, I have answered that question proudly dozens and dozens of times, "Yes!" only to see their expression of love as they signed to me stories about the impact my parents made on them. What were they really saying in short? They were saying, "Your parents gave me hope."

I want to close this chapter with a "how to" regarding using hope language. Let's start with meditation. Meditation is a biblical practice that we do not utilize like we should. Meditation is so powerful and, when used properly, is life changing. Meditation is an act of the mind. Meditation is summed up as continued or extended thought and is also reflection and contemplation. Psalms has a powerful verse in relation to meditation.

My heart was hot within me, while I was musing the fire burned: then spake I with my tongue (Psalm 39:3).

What a verse! Our society has become so a-mused that they have lost the ability to "muse." Musing is meditation and contemplation at its best. Notice the process here. The psalmist says his heart was hot within, then the muse took place, and then he "spake" with his tongue.

Our culture has become less and less about individually motivated meditation and thought, and become more about dependence on letting others think for us. Amusement parks entertain us. The media is constantly telling us how to think. Educational institutions of higher learning feed a lot of naïve robots talking points without giving any thought toward logic and common sense.

Obviously, I am not opposed to much of what we call amusement, but I am concerned about the lack of personal meditation. When one meditates on the blessings of life, we then gain a new perspective and anticipation for future blessings. When we meditate, we become more grateful for the good things of yesterday, we apply them to today, and we alter our tomorrows for the better.

Hopeful language is readily appreciated when one meditates. We reflect on the many times we received hope, and then we help those who may need hope. Hopeful language circulates regularly at church, in the workplace, and even in our own homes when Christians as a whole practice regular meditation. Think on the blessings, joys, and hopes, and then spread the blessings, joys, and hopes. Meditate! Contemplate! Appreciate! Gravitate! Get hope! Give hope!

"Sorry that your child is deaf," said the teacher. "But, don't worry . . . I know a couple named Art and Joyce Dignan who are deaf married adults living the American dream. When your child is older, we can set up a meeting. Don't fret. There is hope."

And he said unto her, Daughter, be of good comfort: thy faith hath made thee whole; go in peace (Luke 8:48).

Jesus, Dad, and Mom—thank you for being givers of hope. There is hope. God is good.

Nine

Music to My Ears

And he saith unto them, Follow me, and I will make you fishers of men (Matthew 4:19).

What a verse! What a statement. Follow me, and I will make you. I am often asked by people if deaf people will be offended if non-deaf try to talk to them. Maybe they will not want a new sign language learner to practice sign language with them. I have a simple response to questions like these.

The deaf have learned to get along just fine in a hearing world. The deaf are used to the majority not understanding them, while the deaf themselves understand the majority quite well.

Several years ago I was speaking at a conference in Chicago when a Romanian friend of mine asked if we could go out to breakfast. I gladly accepted. This gentleman came from behind the communist curtain of Romania years ago and had incredible insight and ideas on freedom and what the United States of America should be paying attention to. In the midst of our conversation, the gentleman apologized to me for his broken English. I encouraged him by reminding him that his English was much better than my Romanian.

I have watched my parents, my sister, and other deaf family and friends adapt to living in a world where the majority of people don't understand the minorities that share the same country as them. On my social media pages, if you look carefully at the comments on many of my posts, you will most likely be able to tell the difference in the comments made by my deaf friends and the comments made by my hearing friends. Why?

Because many of my deaf friends haven't mastered the English language like my hearing friends have. It is easy for someone to ask, "What is wrong with their English?" To which I kindly answer, "My deaf friends use and knowledge of English is better than your use and knowledge of sign language." English, of course, is not the native language of the deaf culture in the United States. I do want to mention that there are many deaf who are amazing English users even though it is their second language.

Harmonious language? What does it mean? Why this chapter, and why now? Jesus came to this earth to infuse harmony between God and man. They had good harmony in the beginning, but that was breached by man's sin. Jesus came to put this relationship back in harmony.

Harmonious simply means marked by agreement in feeling, attitude, and action, and that which is pleasant to the ear. Once again, we see that Jesus, through Heart Language, had a main mission of putting back into harmony and unity the relationship between God and man, but He also in His earthly ministry wanted to be an example to us all in bringing us to harmony.

My wife and children sing a lot as we travel. They sing in such a way that blesses the ear. As they sing about God and

His goodness, it blesses the ear while ministering to the heart. Harmony is when two separate entities, once at odds, are now in agreement again. Jesus was the Master of this.

It did not matter if the parties involved were Jews and Gentiles, Samaritans and Jews, disciples and Pharisees, adults and children, friends and foes—He was able to put back into harmony what once wasn't. He loves to hear harmony now, where once there was none. This chapter challenges us to look at this beautiful concept of harmonious language.

It was January 3, 1997. I was sitting at the table and my palms were sweaty, and the ring was in my left pocket. She was sitting next to me, and her parents were across the table from me. I knew that after the meal was done, I was going to sit on a bench overlooking the city of Huntingdon, Pennsylvania, and I was going to read an eighty-plus line poem that ended with the question, "Will you marry me?"

I read the poem, and thank God, she said, "Yes, I will." That night changed my life forever. Fast-forward to July 5, 1997. That day would be the day that my beautiful Janelle and I would say, "I do." I sure am glad I did. After twenty-plus years together, four children, and twenty-plus years of ministry, she's still my dream, and I love her with every ounce of my being. She truly is the greatest thing to ever happen to me aside from my salvation by Jesus.

What does this have to do with harmonious language? I am so glad you asked. Here were people from two very different worlds that were going to unite in matrimony, and the key to any successful marriage is to maximize the potential harmony.

Janelle grew up in the same town all her life. She attended the same church, the same school, she even lived in the same house in the mountains of central Pennsylvania. She had only ever seen one deaf family in her life before meeting me. If you asked her when she was maybe sixteen years old if she would ever be fluent in American Sign Language, she would probably have given you the kind of smile that I have received many times, which could be interpreted, "What are you talking about?" Kindly, of course.

My story was the complete opposite. Earlier in this book I mentioned my very different upbringing. We lived in multiple states, including twice in California and twice in Florida, and multiple houses. She attended one school her whole life until college, and I on the other hand, attended more than five different schools. She only ever knew of one deaf family growing up. I was around thousands. She lived in a small town tucked away in the mountains of Pennsylvania. I lived in big cities, small cities, the country, the north, the south, the east, and the west. Yet, from July 5, 1997, until now, we have been in harmony. How? Of course our marriage has not been perfect, but we have experienced consistent harmony.

My wife knew before we got married that there was a deaf culture/deaf world background ingrained in me. She understood that it was my life. My family, my upbringing, my friends—much of my life was saturated in the deaf community. I remember my wife noting that the deaf culture couldn't be that much different than her culture and her world.

After a short time of marriage, she came back to me and admitted that she had misjudged because the deaf culture is vastly different. She has since learned sign language and is fluent in it. She emphasized it so much that my children, all four of them, are also fluent in it. She and three of my daughters regularly sign in church, and my son communicates freely with his grandparents, uncle, aunt, and cousins using sign language. How is all of this even possible? How can a lady meet a man, accept his proposal, and then live a life that harmonizes beautifully two worlds and two cultures?

This brings us to our opening verse.

And he saith unto them, Follow me, and I will make you fishers of men (Matthew 4:19).

Follow me. What a simple statement. Put yourself in the shoes of the disciple right now and imagine a man walking up to you and saying these two simple words. Eight letters, two words, three total syllables, and you leave everything you've known all your life and you follow Him.

The word "follow" is the backbone of harmonious language. Follow is a beautiful word. Follow simply means to come after in sequence or order; to conform or comply with. When Jesus said, "Follow me," He didn't just mean, "Listen to what I say"; He was also saying, "Watch what I do, observe how I live, and learn how I engage."

Following is something we do all the time without regular realization. We follow our schedule, we follow our roads, we follow traffic, we follow the traffic lights, we follow the clock, we follow our coworkers, we follow our leadership, we follow and we follow.

By definition, we follow more than we realize. I think many times we think of following as a classroom of kindergarteners standing behind and in front of their classmates as they head out to recess. In actuality, the word follow is so much more.

Following is the key to harmonious language, and following also includes a powerful word—willingness. My wife had to be willing to follow or conform and comply to deaf culture. The disciples had to follow or conform and comply to the life Jesus was trying to demonstrate to them. Jesus was a Man of action. He was a leader who was willing to walk His talk. We live in a time when many leaders talk a good talk, but Heart Language leaders will walk the walk.

The old saying goes like this, "Your talk talks, and your walk talks, but your walk talks louder than your talk talks." My wife, like Jesus, was willing to abide by another vital principle, "When in Rome, do as the Romans do." Jesus was willing to go through Samaria, He was willing to pay attention to the children, He was willing to help lepers, and He was willing to care for the sick. Jesus, the great leader, was willing to "follow" or conform and comply to the very needs of the people He ministered to. The greatest leaders remain the greatest followers as well.

My wife amazes me in this area of harmonious language. She understands that her husband has a bicultural, bilingual approach to this life. She sees that in order to follow and live out harmonious language, she had to suspend some of her traditional mindsets, consistent upbringing, and instilled stereotypes to embrace a vastly different culture and language.

She has passed that on to our four children. I could not have done this without her. My four children have been privileged to grow up bicultural and bilingual because my wife promoted harmonious language. My children amaze me as well, as all four of them are fluent users of sign language, and more importantly, harmonious language. Briella, Rayana,

Grant, and Clara—thank you so much for being living evidence of harmonious language and loving it as well.

If you are an American reading this right now, here is something to think about—God is not an American. What does this mean? Well, I have heard it often asked like this. If you know three languages, what are you? Trilingual. If you know two languages, what are you? Bilingual. If you only know one language, what are you? American. How true this is!

As Americans, we think Christianity should be done the American way. OK, what is that? Please define this for me. When you go to a deaf church, hold a revival in the Bahamas, go on a mission trip to the Philippines, or speak at a conference in Ecuador, you'll realize the rest of this world did not get the American memo.

The music is different outside America, the food is different, the culture is different, the language is different, and the way they conduct church services is very different—so what do you do? You harmonize. You comply and you conform. You follow even though you may be leading.

This applies to the business world as well. If you are the president of a company or the CEO, follow your management as you lead them. If you are in management for a company or a place of business, follow your employees. If you are an employee, follow the customer.

What does this all mean? Harmonious language makes the best leaders the best followers as they lead their followers. I know this sounds odd, but how true it is and how powerful it can be when applied.

My wife was willing to follow the deaf world in harmony and is still making a difference in the deaf world today. Jesus, the greatest leader ever, followed all of His followers. He complied to their needs and conformed to their problems because He mastered bringing them to harmony with Him. When music is in harmony, when a family is in harmony, when a business is in harmony, when a church is in harmony, it sure is music to the ears of all who listen and observe.

I have spent time overseas on mission trips, I regularly speak in jails and prisons, I travel and speak in the northwest, the northeast, the southwest, the southeast, and everywhere in between. What have I learned?

One major thing I have learned is that Heart Language sets the stage for harmonious language, and it becomes an amazing unifier of two entities that started out incompatible at first.

Harmonious language can even make two leaders follow each other as they both lead in ministry. While many lean on me for leadership and guidance and teaching, I have learned so much from my followers.

Harmonious language helps us recognize that even the senior saint in a nursing home can add value because of harmonious language, as well as a toddler. I have learned so much as a leader from my many followers because I have learned the power of harmonious language. Trust me, I have failed many times, and I will continue to do so, but think of all the work that can get done—the bridge building, the love, the unification—when we begin to regularly use harmonious language.

Let's say a CEO sits down with a ground-level employee and asks, "What is it like where you are at? How is your work going? Are you able to maximize and reach your full potential?" What if that same CEO, who leads the company, learns what it is really like, and complies and conforms and makes a difference to that employee and even to the company? What if?

What if politicians who are supposed to be leaders of their constituents genuinely listened to their leaders and became followers via harmonious language? What if the politicians complied and conformed to what was presented to them?

Little do we realize that we will become much better leaders when we become better followers. The gap is narrowed, and the divide is connected by harmonious language. Because my wife was willing to embrace harmonious language, and my children were as well, we can all now sit down at a meal and use the language of our choice to communicate. And when we are around our dear deaf family, we are all able to harmonize, communicate, and enjoy each other's company. Why? Harmonious language is the difference maker.

Jesus wanted His disciples to truly understand that a genuine leader is willing to "follow" his/her followers to become the leaders they were destined to be. The following is a simple example of how we might use harmonious language in our daily lives without realizing it.

My family and I love to go to the zoo. My children are much older now, but when they were smaller, they would follow my wife and me all over the zoo. We were the leaders, and they were the followers. I remember many times having one of my children ask, "Daddy, can you pick me up? I can't see the bears." Of course, I picked them up. I conformed to their request. I harmonized with their need. I went to their level and brought them up to mine.

I, as their leader, their daddy, was presented a need, and

we harmonized. They saw the bears clearly, and I conformed to their needs. Leaders would do well to realize that the reason we are leaders is because there are needs from our followers. A leader is supposed to be out front and paving the way, but when the leaders don't stop, look back, and check up on their followers, they lose valuable opportunities for harmonious language.

Maybe that is why there are so many boss/employee jokes, and most of them are not so flattering. Maybe, just maybe, this is the reason there are so many mother-in-law jokes. The old in-law clash is still real today. Harmonious language can help that out.

Harmonious language is truly the bridge between leaders and followers, and followers and leaders. In many instances, from the business world, to the church, to Main Street, people forget where they came from or even lose touch, so there is no harmony between two separate parties that in reality need proper understanding of each other to better work together.

Jesus was the Master of this. He went everywhere living Heart Language and teaching harmonious language. He ministered to all sorts. He understood their every individual need. He ministered to those needs. He, the greatest leader who ever lived, became the greatest follower who ever lived by surrendering His life on the cross so that we might follow Him to heaven through the amazing gift of salvation.

Jesus used harmonious language to unite certain Pharisees with the common folk. He used harmonious language to unite the Samaritans with the Jews. He used harmonious language to unite the Jews with the Gentiles. He used harmonious language to unite the disciples. He used harmonious language to unite Saul, later Paul, to Himself.

Jesus used harmonious language to unite mankind to God the Father once again. Jesus uses harmonious language every day in our lives to unite us to His ways. Wow! What a leader! Wow! What a follower! Jesus uses harmonious language to this day to help us unite to Him as husbands, fathers, wives, mothers, sons, daughters, and Christians.

The chapter started off with the question I receive from well-meaning nondeaf folk on a regular basis. "Can I approach a deaf person?" "Will they get mad if I bother them?" "Will deaf people be OK with me practicing sign language with them?" "Will deaf people get offended at me because I don't understand them?"

All of these questions originate from well-meaning thought. Allow me to encourage you by saying that the deaf regularly embrace and are even excited many times when someone from the majority world temporarily shines a spotlight on their minority world. Go ahead, try it, harmonize. The deaf are actually the better half of the harmony at first in many relationships. Lead. Follow. Follow. Lead. Comply. Conform. Agree. Harmonize. It is possible. It takes two to tango, and it takes two to harmonize.

Jesus and Janelle, thank you both for being amazing examples of consistent harmonious language. Briella, Rayana, Grant, and Clara, thank you as well. When harmonious language is used regularly, it become music to our ears and a sight for sore eyes. Try it! Harmonize! You won't be sorry.

Whoever you are and wherever you are, use harmonious language with somebody right now. Comply, conform, and agree. Learn when it is necessary to lead then follow, or follow then lead. Harmonious language will help us with this important part of our lives. Let's do it. Let's use harmonious language to harmonize.

Ten

I Can't Lift This

He went away again the second time, and prayed, saying,
O my Father, if this cup may not pass away from me, ex-
cept I drink it, thy will be done (Matthew 26:42).

The morning of this writing started out usual for me. I got up. I went to the family room of our basement. I read my Bible. I meditated. I prayed. I read over my goals. I went to our makeshift gym that connects outside and started my workout. It was early, and the sun was just beginning to shine.

I got to the back patio and began to do some push-ups, and I heard the activity of my environment. I heard the birds singing. I heard the squirrels running, climbing, and jumping through the trees. I heard cars driving in the distance and leaves moving as commanded by the breeze. I heard roofers. I heard the sounds of life as I was progressing through my workout.

My father and my mother have never heard these sounds. They have never heard a bird sing or a dog faintly barking in the neighborhood. Stop what you are doing right now and just listen. Hear the sounds of the world, the sounds of life.

Heavy language. What is it? It is language that is hard, hurtful, or difficult to understand at times. To many who read the previous paragraphs, the normal response would be sympathy. Imagine never hearing music, the laughter of a baby, or the sounds of a loved one saying, "I love you." My parents have never heard all of the above. You say, "That's heavy." Yes, it is. However, I have never seen my parents complain about it one time. Not once.

This chapter is an important one regarding Heart Language because we all have experienced heavy language, are experiencing it, or will sometime in our life. This book has been, for the most part, upbeat and positive, but we cannot disregard the fact that life does bring us bad news and bad experiences from time to time. It could be one phone call that changes our lives. It could be a simple visit to a doctor. It could also be a great loss.

Life will deal us heavy situations and news we think is too heavy for us to lift. This is where Heart Language can help us with heavy language. My father and mother chose to love their life and realized that somebody else out there always has it heavier than they do. I observed a positive outlook all my life from my deaf parents and my deaf sister, for which I am so proud of them.

I obviously do not want to send a message that we all should deal with heavy language through Heart Language and just go on with life. The contrary is the purpose of this chapter. Because of Heart Language, we can deal with heavy language. Heart Language is the foundation on which we can stand when heavy language tries to knock us down.

The old saying, "It's all in how you look at it," can definitely be applied to this chapter. My father and mother often teased that thunderstorms, or sirens, or annoying dogs barking never bothered them at night. How true that is! We all can look at our own lives and see the complexity, the heaviness, and we can turn it into a blessing and help others with whom we cross paths.

Jesus faced something heavy. He faced something no man would ever be able to face. He was about to lift something so heavy, all mankind together would not be able to lift it. He, who knew no sin, was to become sin for us. He was to experience separation from His Father and a forsaking like none before. He was to pick something up so that we all would always have help with our many "heavies" of life.

Jesus had a mission, and His mission was to lift the heavy. In fact, He was to lift the heaviest of heavies. He was to experience something no other man would ever be able to endure so that we could look to Him as an example, a pattern on how to carry our heavies of life well.

Jesus put others first, and that is the key to dealing with heavy language. I remember observing from a distance one time, a robin defending its nest against a much larger predatory bird. That robin was willing to die for the nest because of its contents—the baby birds. They became the robin's motivation in the heavy situation.

Life is not a bed of roses. It is difficult. It is complex, and there will be times, many times, we do not understand why something is happening to us. Our loved ones will embrace heavy times and situations, and we will even feel helpless. This is where Heart Language comes in.

Let us break down the following verse and try to understand heavy language.

*He went away again the second time, and prayed, saying,
O my Father, if this cup may not pass away from me, except I drink it, thy will be done* (Matthew 26:42).

First of all, notice the usage of the word cup. A cup?
What does that really mean? A cup is an object that is either
one of two things—a container that is either empty or one
that is holding contents. In life we all are assigned cups. Cups
come in different sizes, and they serve different purposes.
Some cups are better for cold beverages, others for hot. Some
cups are decorative, others are there to serve a practical purpose.

We all carry different cups throughout our lives.
Sometimes they change, and there are times when the contents of our cup are sweet. Maybe we got a new job, a raise, or
a baby was born. The contents of these cups of life are
pleasant and enjoyable.

Other times we taste the contents from our cups of life,
and they taste bitter, sour, and disheartening. We all know
that medicine doesn't always taste good, but it is necessary.
Ecclesiastes 3 shows the contrasts of life well. There is a time
to be born and a time to die. There is a time to weep and a
time to laugh. Eight powerful verses in that chapter remind
us of the many cups of life.

We all will have times and seasons where we feel as if
what we carry is so heavy that we cannot go on. It is at these
times we will survive because of Heart Language. Jesus became the master Teacher of this, and He became our chief
example.

Jesus carried His cup so others would have help for all of
their cups of life. Jesus was so driven by Heart Language, He

embraced a cup and its contents that were specifically designed for Him. He carried it and drank of it so that we may all be able to handle our cups.

True Christianity is about others. When we learn to put others first because of our understanding of Heart Language, we then begin to comprehend the purposes for our many cups of life. Jesus said it best in John 9:1–3.

And as Jesus passed by, he saw a man which was blind from his birth. And his disciples asked him, saying, Master, who did sin, this man, or his parents, that he was born blind? Jesus answered, Neither hath this man sinned, nor his parents: but that the works of God should be made manifest in him.

Wow! What a passage. That the works of God should be made manifest in him. God has a specific plan for all. What is so powerful about this is that everyone is unique to God. In that unique design, you and God in the intimacies and depths of your relationship will share things that no one else can.

That's why this blind man, my deaf parents, and Jesus Himself all had unique cups to drink with the potential to share the ups and downs, pain and blessings, and ultimately Heart Language with everyone they met. Living through and with heavy language is an evident way to show a life guided by the principles of Heart Language. Remember that the bottom-line vision and purpose of this book is to make a difference in someone else's life, and that, my friend, is genuine Christianity.

Next, notice the phrase, "If this cup may not pass away from me, except I drink it." This is so powerful. Once again, as heavy language comes our way, whether we are born with it or we have an appointment with it in our lives, Jesus becomes an amazing example for permission to discuss this with God.

Remember, Jesus was 100% God and 100% man at the same time. This is the human side coming out in full force. Jesus is saying that He would rather not drink the contents of this cup because He knew what He was to endure. This leads to the final statement of observation regarding heavy language.

Jesus says, "Thy will be done." When Heart Language courses through our spiritual veins, we will embrace the will of our Father regardless of the circumstances of whatever heavy language we face or endure in our lives. The beauty of this design and cycle is that it is guaranteed to help someone else. Because Jesus drank of His cup, we have salvation and eternal life. My parents embraced their cup and have helped thousands of other deaf individuals, young and old.

Allow me to be an open book at this moment, no pun intended. Many CODAs (children of deaf adults) will read this book. As they do, they will relate to the many stories that have been shared. Let me first say, being a CODA was not easy. I know many CODAs who are bitter, frustrated, and upset at their lot in life.

I remember interpreting phone calls at a young age, when my prepubescent voice begged the person on the other end of the call not to hang up because, as I said to the caller, "I am calling for my dad who is deaf." I remember phone calls that lasted over an hour many times. I remember the schoolyard fights because my deaf parents were being made fun of. I remember trying to explain my home life and family situation countless times to ignorant peers, teachers, and many adults.

I'll admit, it wasn't always easy. One of my cups early on was to be born into a situation that less than two percent of this world will ever experience. I had a choice. I had to decide if I would look at that cup and despise its contents, or look at my cup and learn to love the contents. My father and mother definitely helped with this decision, but it was still my final decision to make. All my life I have heard statements like these:

"Oh my. You poor child. Your parents are deaf."
"Who will keep your house safe at night from criminals? Your parents can't hear them breaking in!"
"You poor thing! I can't imagine not being able to talk to my parents on the phone."
"Your poor parents. They have never heard music. My oh my!"
"Don't you wish your parents were blind instead?"
"How did your poor mother hear you crying in the middle of the night?"
"Who will help you in school with your work?"
"Will you have to live with your parents all your life to help them?"

I could go on and on with many other questions and comments I heard through the years. I could've allowed these sayings and the outlook of society in general to view my cup as one that holds the bitter taste of coffee. I remember early on in my life deciding that I would refuse to focus on the potential for bitterness but rather embrace the sweetness that was there as well. My cup became a cup of good ole sweet tea.

The point of this is that we all have unique stories. We all have things happen in our lives even from the earliest of ages that could appear as heavy. We go through life and things happen. Life happens. A phone call changes everything. There's a big move across the country because of a job change. There's a sick loved one or a tragic death in the family. There's hurt feelings from a bad church experience. Moral decline in society that robs our lives of innocence and purity. Life is not always easy.

In fact, life can be downright mean and hard. The cups come and they go. One week we feel as though there is no heavy language. The very next we struggle trying to make reason of it all. I often say, "Every day we have many reasons to be mad and bitter, but we have just as many reasons to be happy and sweet. We must make the right choice."

Heavy language will come and go, but my joy may remain, and my smile shall be unwavering. Yes, my parents are deaf. Yes, my sister is as well. Five long generations of deafness in my family, and you know what? I love it! I thank God daily for this amazing opportunity. I get to be different from 98 percent of the world.

All of us right now can make the choice to be like Jesus, to be like my deaf dad and deaf mom. We can say, "I did not choose my cups, but I do choose to trust in God and ask Him to help me help others all while having joy in my life." What an example Jesus was and is. What a blessing to read about my parents in this book and think of the many overcomers in this life.

You can do it! I can do it! We all can do it! We can embrace heavy language because, as we start to lift the situation up and carry it, Heart Language comes up right beside us and whispers in our ear and says, "You can do it. I know you can, and I'll be with you all the way."

Heart language also says, "Look at Jesus. Look at Paul. Look at the millions of others who bore their crosses in life and drank of their cups and are now remembered as difference makers." All my life Heart Language has said to me, "Randy, look at the man you call Dad. Look at the lady you call Mom. They have embraced their cups of life and do so with a smile. If they can do it, you can too."

In life we will want to scream out, "I can't lift this." Remember, though, that you can and you must. As a result, you will make a difference in somebody else's life. To my precious Jesus and to my amazing dad and mom, thank you for showing us all that with Heart Language, you can drink of the cups in life and you will make it.

Eleven

Everybody Needs a Hero

Verily, verily, I say unto you, He that believeth on me, the works that I do shall he do also; and greater works than these shall he do; because I go unto my Father (John 14:12).

To be a hero. Movies and the entertainment industry have made billions from the portrayal, in most cases, of a fictitious hero who saves the day. We all know the plot. The story starts out good and introduces the theme to us. A villain shows up and things get bad, but before you see the famed phrase "The End," the hero shows up and saves the day.

A hero is simply defined as a person noted for courageous acts or nobility of character, one who has special achievements, abilities, and is regarded as a role model. We all know there is no real Superman, Captain America, or even the Incredible Hulk. However, we see heroes among us every day.

A hero is not necessarily an athlete or a politician. It is for sure not an actor or an actress. Yet, this crowd seems to get revered as heroes on a regular basis. We idolize and throw money at athletes, actors, and political so-called leaders as if they are heroes. In my humble opinion, in almost all cases, they are not.

A hero is a teacher in a classroom, a fireman finishing up a twenty-four-hour shift, or a doctor who just performed his fifth bypass of the week. A hero is a policeman helping out a domestic dispute, a soldier who misses another Thanksgiving with family because he is overseas again, and a country preacher who barely has enough money to live but serves that rural population of folk who need a pastor.

A hero is a missionary in a foreign land, an EMT jumping on a speeding ambulance to save another life, and a mother who homeschools her children. We run into heroes daily, and in fact many of us have the opportunity to regularly be a hero by definition. Think of someone you know right now who is a hero.

You may also have been a hero to somebody else. Everybody needs a hero, and we all need to be heroes too. History contains many stories of heroes down through the ages, and their stories consist of people who did amazing things for other people. They performed courageous acts and exhibited nobility of character. The Bible records many of them, and our history books tell of their deeds.

The greatest hero of all, of course, is Jesus Christ. His courageous acts and His nobility of character are peppered throughout the Gospels, and even John said that the books of this world could not contain all that Jesus did. His life of Heart Language made Him a hero time and time again.

To the deaf world, Arthur Dignan is a hero. To the deaf child, Joyce Dignan is a hero. To the three children who called them Dad and Mom, the Dignans are heroes. I know as my brother Nick and my sister Jennifer read these words, they will echo this sentiment.

You see, anyone can be a hero. Are you a parent? Do you love your child or children? Do you desire to live out Heart Language? If you answered yes to all of these questions as I do, then you are a hero. Heroes are more common than we realize, and we need to make much ado of true heroes and watch the daily impacts they can make on this world.

Entertainment heroes are far different than engagement heroes. Heroes who daily engage in the lives of others are the real life changers. Think right now about a hero you had in your life by definition, and think about what made them a hero to you specifically. It amazes me how many successful athletes thank a parent, a coach, or a teacher for helping them get where they are in life.

Our opening verse is a powerful verse that should excite us with the potential of it. Jesus says if we believe on Him, we will see greater works. Works? What works? The labors, the deeds, and even the toils of Christ and His ministry is what is meant. Every fictitious hero has labors, deeds, and toils that must take place so that they might overcome and be a hero.

Jesus was living proof of that. He labored and toiled and walked this earth, teaching and performing miracle after miracle. He was in the truest form a difference maker. Then Jesus says that we can do the same works and even greater works. How exciting!

Everybody needs a hero from time to time, and in that need we realize that a true hero helps us better ourselves in this life. A true hero goes out of his way to make sure your life is safe, cared for, and even improved. This is why I can say with all gladness that anybody can be a hero. Heroes are heroes for different reasons and purposes for all kinds of people and their many situations and circumstances of life.

The art of being a hero is encouraging because anybody who exercises Heart Language will find themselves in a beautiful cycle of needing a hero one day and being a hero the next. I grew up observing my parents as heroes. They were difference makers in the lives of scores of other deaf people, mostly younger than them. Their selfless acts and nobility of character are still talked about to this day.

Let's shift our focus to the how-to of Heart Language and hero language now. As we continue to live out the principles of Heart Language, we will begin to see doors open up for opportunities to be somebody's hero while noticing our own heroes. This cycle is why Christianity is still going strong two thousand years since Jesus Christ lived.

In the famous story of David killing Goliath in 1 Samuel 17, we see a young man who was simply obeying his father and brought some food to his big brothers on a distant battlefield. His arrival could not have been more timely. He showed up at just the right time. One hillside contained a confident enemy, while the other held a fearful band of soldiers. David stood up and stood out. The rest is history. David became a hero that day and made many heroes that day as well.

You may be thinking that this is a war story, so of course it demands a hero. How about the book of Exodus? The common hero of that book is a man named Moses. Think about the fact that there would be no Moses to help deliver Israel from Egypt if not for a mother who boldly risked everything, including her own life, so that Moses would survive the massacre ordered by Pharaoh.

We all agree that Jesus is the greatest hero of all. Take note that Jesus needed a mother named Mary and an earthly father named Joseph who had to overcome ceremonial customs and even laws to obey God all the way to a stable where the King would be born. Joseph and Mary, fluent in Heart Language, were also hero language users as well.

Paul is often considered the hero of the Gentile church. He traveled the known world at that time and started churches, endured persecution and imprisonment, and preached over and over. He wrote much of the New Testament. Yet, without the heroes Ananias and Barnabas, we may never have known the beloved Paul.

We should be seeing a trend here. A true hero acts in the best interest of another party. I wonder how many professional athletes would still play their sport if they were paid the same salary as a soldier. Would a politician do the same work if their salary was that of a teacher? Please do not misunderstand me. Having been one who played athletics at a high level and engages in politics regularly, I am not on a crusade against these two groups. Rather, I just want to define a hero as clearly as possible.

Actors and actresses make millions, and, granted, their work is sometimes hard, but is it really heroic? The trend that we established with David; Jochebed, the mother of Moses; Mary; Joseph; Ananias; and Barnabas is simply this: their heroic acts were done for somebody else.

Much of who society considers to be a hero today is backward according to the definition of hero in its truest form. Legit heroes will always put others above themselves. Heroes go out of their way to better someone else even if it means an inconvenience to them. They show love in action and display altruistic tendencies on a regular basis.

That's why we can include dads, moms, policemen,

firemen, teachers, principals, doctors, nurses, preachers, Sunday school teachers, deacons, elders, and next-door neighbors.

Unfortunately, the resume for a hero has been hijacked and rewritten. Modern-day applications for heroes require athleticism, intelligence, good looks, amazing charisma, fame, and even wealth. The emphasis on heroes of today comes from how much they can entertain us. This definition of heroism is far from the life of Heart Language. I do know many engage in philanthropy, and that is great; but when we emphasize heroism without Heart Language, it puts becoming a hero out of reach for all.

Historic and even biblical definitions of the word hero have an all-inclusive application. In other words, "Apply inside, heroes needed." This means that you—yes you—can be and should be a hero. It means I can as well. The world is looking for genuine heroes, and Heart Language is the highway upon which hero language can transport itself regularly.

Back to our verse to start this chapter. Jesus uses the word "works." He then says greater works will be done. Do we realize the power of this? Each and every day of our lives can be spent looking for heroes and being heroes. Everybody needs a hero from time to time.

To a child growing up in a single-parent home, you—that's right, you Sunday school teacher or youth pastor or football coach—you can be that child's hero. To many children across this country, even with all the dangerous influences out there, some people are still governed by Heart Language and become a hero on a daily basis.

Please understand that we are not heroes first and then

participate in heroic activities. Rather, we participate in heroic activities and then we become heroes. The church I pastor is full of heroes. We have a deaf couple that drives a van and picks up deaf folk every week, and the drive time adds a good two hours to their Sunday routine. Heroes! We have a young couple that weekly visits children and then brings them to church on a bus and teaches them about Jesus. Heroes!

We have many Sunday school teachers who spend time weekly in study, preparation, and visiting of their classes. Heroes! We have many volunteers that go into juvenile centers, jails, and prisons week in and week out to teach and preach the Bible. Heroes! I could go on and on. America was liberated by heroes, has been sustained by heroes, and will continue because of heroes.

This chapter is unique because it has actually been less about my parents and even Jesus and more about you and me becoming heroes because we have Heart Language. You and I are here today because of heroes, and it is now our time to be the heroes our society needs.

As we wrap up this chapter, let us see the results of those that live out Heart Language and embrace the how of hero language. Moses is born, and God uses him to deliver the children of Israel. A young man takes a slingshot and five smooth stones and becomes an inspiration to a whole nation for generations to come.

A man named Saul becomes a man named Paul, and we still talk about him two thousand years later. Every year families and churches gather to celebrate the birth of the Son of God, the Savior of mankind. The heroes of the Bible are heroes because they did heroic things. Hang in there, Dad. You are making a difference! Do not give up, Mom on that child who really matters. Stay after it, teacher. You just never know what that one student may become someday.

Some may be heroes to thousands. Some may be heroes to just a few. Some may just be a hero to even one, but a hero is a hero is a hero. The measure of a hero is not in the numbers of people that deem one a hero, but rather it is in the changed life that results because of a hero, whether it is one or many. Thank God for heroes.

So my parents were heroes to many thousands of deaf children, teens, and even adults. Jesus was and is a hero to millions upon millions. When all is said and done, my parents and Jesus are heroes to me—yes, me—the individual who needed a hero. Thank you, Dad! Thank you, Mom! Thank You, Jesus! Because of your Heart Language, I heard your hero language loud and clear exactly when I needed it.

Twelve

Ticket for Final Destination

For God so loved the world, that he gave his only begotten Son, that whosoever believeth in him should not perish, but have everlasting life (John 3:16).

The single most famous verse in the Bible is no doubt John 3:16. There are many other famous passages of Scripture, but none quite like John 3:16. This verse that is known and loved by the masses was quoted to one person, by Jesus Himself, in the middle of the night. This verse was not proclaimed in a massive crowd, or at the feeding of the thousands, or even to His own disciples. John 3:16 was shared with one person, and this blessed individual's name was Nicodemus. Here is the passage leading up to the famous verse.

> *There was a man of the Pharisees, named Nicodemus, a ruler of the Jews: The same came to Jesus by night, and said unto him, Rabbi, we know that thou art a teacher come from God: for no man can do these miracles that thou doest, except God be with him.*
> *Jesus answered and said unto him, Verily, verily, I say*

unto thee, Except a man be born again, he cannot see the kingdom of God. Nicodemus saith unto him, How can a man be born when he is old? can he enter the second time into his mother's womb, and be born?

Jesus answered, Verily, verily, I say unto thee, Except a man be born of water and of the Spirit, he cannot enter into the kingdom of God. That which is born of the flesh is flesh; and that which is born of the Spirit is spirit. Marvel not that I said unto thee, Ye must be born again. The wind bloweth where it listeth, and thou hearest the sound thereof, but canst not tell whence it cometh, and whither it goeth: so is every one that is born of the Spirit.

Nicodemus answered and said unto him, How can these things be?

Jesus answered and said unto him, Art thou a master of Israel, and knowest not these things? Verily, verily, I say unto thee, We speak that we do know, and testify that we have seen; and ye receive not our witness If I have told you earthly things, and ye believe not, how shall ye believe, if I tell you of heavenly things? And no man hath ascended up to heaven, but he that came down from heaven, even the Son of man which is in heaven. And as Moses lifted up the serpent in the wilderness, even so must the Son of man be lifted up: That whosoever believeth in him should not perish, but have eternal life. For God so loved the world, that he gave his only begotten Son, that whosoever believeth in him should not perish, but have everlasting life (John 3:1–16).

What a passage! What a story! What an event! Imagine being there and listening to these two religious legends discuss the weighty issues of spirituality and the things of God. Nicodemus, as described, was a man of influence, a Pharisee, a ruler of the Jews. He sets up a meeting with Jesus, and the rest is history.

The statement is made that they met by night. Jesus was already shaping up to be a controversial figure, and Nicodemus knew that a daytime meeting might compromise his standing in the eyes of his many contemporaries. We have the awesome privilege of seeing Jesus exercise Heart Language in their conversation. Heart Language can and should eventually express heavenly language, the emphasis of this chapter.

The critics of Jesus often point out that He accepted this meeting because of Nicodemus and his power and influence. We see the name of Nicodemus written in this chapter, and John, who wrote this book, made sure that we knew Jesus met with Nicodemus. However, as you read through John, you will see Jesus meeting one-on-one with others whose names aren't even mentioned.

The very next chapter He meets with the person who is commonly known as "the woman at the well." He then goes on to meet the man by the pool of Bethesda. He meets with the young lad and uses his lunch to feed the multitudes. He meets with the woman caught in the act of adultery. He has some one-on-one time with the blind man, who of course Jesus heals. Jesus shows Himself as not a respecter of persons. He was willing always to meet with anybody one-on-one because His desire to live out and use Heart Language would eventually lead to heavenly language conversation.

Jesus knew eternal life was and is real. He knew that He would desire to challenge conventional thinking on the afterlife and present what He said as truth, everlasting life. As part of the eternal Godhead, He came to earth as temporal man to give us temporal people hope of eternal life. This language that Jesus presents to us and speaks to us is a heavenly language.

This heavenly language breaks us away from the here and now and causes us to pause and think on eternal matters. The age-old debate has been and will continue to be the afterlife. Is there life after death? Is there a heaven? Is there a hell? Jesus earned the right to speak on these matters and validate all of His teachings because He experienced the common death of man, and then three days later, embraced the extremely uncommon resurrection. More on this in a bit.

I have a memory from the 1970s. My mother and father were married in June 1972. My mother, as mentioned before, came from the state of Ohio and from a completely deaf family. Her mother and father were deaf, as well as her older brother John and her younger brother Raymond. I have always loved and admired my uncle John and my uncle Raymond. My mother and my uncles, on their father's side, had many deaf family members.

On their mother's side, however, were mostly hearing people. They had a cousin named Norman that I have met several times. He was hearing and knew some sign language, but not much. In the 1970s, obviously, no such technological benefits existed like email, texting, FaceTime, and the like. Most communication, especially for the deaf, was by good, old-fashioned snail mail. Norman had experienced salvation and became born again. He immediately got burdened for his deaf cousin Raymond and handwrote a letter to my uncle Raymond, explaining the importance of experiencing personal salvation and trusting Christ for forgiveness and redemption. Not long after, my uncle Raymond was converted and became a Christian. Thank God.

In the later part of the 1970s, my uncle Raymond visited his sister Joyce and his brother-in-law, Arthur, my parents. He explained to them the need for personal salvation and, thank God, my parents received Jesus and His redemptive salvation as well.

From Jesus talking to Nicodemus, and Norman talking to Raymond, and Raymond talking to Arthur and Joyce, we see the power of love and heavenly language. By the way, my uncle Raymond has been serving God as a missionary in South America, ministering in three different countries for almost forty years. He pastors a church and runs a school for the deaf. He loves people, travels all over, visits people, and uses a heavenly language. He is my hero, and I thank God for my deaf missionary uncle who is an expert at heavenly language.

This is so important to me because I eventually understood heavenly language at the age of eighteen and received Christ's gift of personal salvation as well. Now let's pause. You may ask why I waited until I was eighteen. That is a great question. You see, I was sprinkled as a baby, baptized three different times growing up, but I never personally understood salvation until later in life.

The reason for this may sound controversial, but truth is at times controversial. Because my parents are deaf, the only churches we attended during my growing-up years were churches that offered deaf ministries. While I am grateful for their attempts to minister to the deaf, I rarely if ever heard heavenly language.

Here is where it gets controversial, but please understand where I am coming from. Not all churches speak or use heavenly language. The reason for that is that many of them do not speak or use Heart Language. Think about this for a bit. Just because a sign has the word "church" on it does not mean it practices what the Bible truly teaches about eternal life. Just because people set aside a few hours on Sunday morning to attend does not mean their churches use or speak heavenly language.

This, my friend, is why Jesus was so controversial. He challenged traditional religion; He combatted determined religious leaders and taught the confused masses. Remember, the truth apologizes to no man, and heavenly language is language that will speak truth. As was mentioned already, we want doctors, dentists, certified public accountants, and financial planners to tell us the truth. If they don't, we set about finding another one straightaway.

Yet, the masses sit in churches because they've always done it, and in many instances never stop and ask themselves if they are being taught the truth about eternity and heavenly language. I would hope that all would want to hear the truth clearly at least once so that they can make a personal decision regarding the truth.

There are so many religions today. There are so many Christian branches, and branches off the bigger branches, and so on. So like Nicodemus, we all need to come to grips with eternity and recognize it is a one-on-one conversation and then a personal decision.

When Nicodemus came to Jesus, he called Him "Rabbi" and then made a simple statement about the miracles of Jesus. Jesus immediately answers the real question at hand by making the statement twice in a span of five verses, "Ye must be born again." Jesus explains that in order to get to the Kingdom of God, one must be born again.

Heavenly language is the culmination of all the languages of this book, with Heart Language at its foundation. Heavenly language gives our temporal lives a peek at eternal living. Heavenly language compels us to ponder our spiritual well-being and final eternal destination. Heavenly language may appear somewhat controversial, but when used properly, is fueled by love. Heavenly language is not a matter of life and death but rather afterlife and death.

Heavenly language brings about spiritual connotations to a very physical realm. We now begin to understand the terminology of Jesus, "Ye must be born again." He is shifting to heavenly, spiritual conversation using a physical understanding. We all know what it means to be born. We all have physical birthdays. As you are reading this book right now, you are a certain age in life because on a particular day of a particular month of a particular year, you were born.

This brings us to the wisdom of Jesus. He knows He is in the physical realm and speaking in a human body, but He also knows that the kingdom of God is not of this same physical realm. He knows this kingdom represents the spiritual, the never dying part of a being. Jesus knew we would all relate to physical birth.

The response of Nicodemus to Jesus stating that we all must be born again is proof that Nicodemus understood the physical birth but not quite the spiritual birth. You see, heavenly language teaches the powerful truth that man needs two births. The physical birth—we all have that—and the spiritual birth—we do not all have that. This is the why of Jesus and His mission to die on the cross and live again for us. His death would pay for our sins; His life would give us a newness of living in the spiritual realm. The death of Jesus cleanses and forgives us, and the resurrection of Jesus enables us and gives us the unlimited, eternal spiritual life before us.

The chapter started with Nicodemus and Jesus, then went to my uncle Raymond and his cousin, then to my parents, and now we see what heavenly language can do. This is just amazing! Jesus was not speaking English to Nicodemus. My uncle Raymond's cousin wrote him a letter in English. My uncle Raymond shared the Gospel with my parents in American Sign Language.

In all instances, heavenly language was used. Going back to the beginning of the book, Heart Language to now—heavenly language goes beyond English, French, Russian, American Sign Language, Spanish, Mandarin, and all the other languages of this planet.

Heart Language and heavenly language combine to be the language of the soul. It is not written, read, seen, or heard, but rather sensed, felt, known, and touched. It is genuine concern, it is love, understanding, sympathy, and even empathy. Heavenly language goes beyond the limitations of language barriers and cultural misunderstandings; rather, it parks in the neighborhood of genuine depth and bonding. This is what separates Jesus from all religious leaders of His day. This is what made Jesus so special that we still sing and speak of Him today. This is why everything shuts down in many countries on this planet on His birthday—because Jesus mastered Heart Language and wants all of us to strive to understand it.

When it comes to spiritual matters, man does a bit too

much interjecting. Man has added so much to what Jesus said about salvation and what it entails. Man has a burning desire to add to what Jesus did for us.

Heart Language and heavenly language take Jesus at face value and recognize that what Jesus wanted us to believe is made clear in the famous verse, John 3:16. If you notice, I have kept this book on a more positive, uplifting level, but it is necessary to see that the enemy of Christianity desires confusion. Confusion is a horrible place to learn from, especially in relation to spiritual matters.

If we can be confused about the truth, we will not be able to understand what is truth. Confusion borderlines on simple twists of words and additions of doctrine; in many cases, it becomes a cloudy lie. Jesus makes it pretty clear in this passage that when we are born again and believe on the Son of God, everlasting life is gifted to us.

Genuine heavenly language teaches all that salvation is a gift, not a reward. A reward is something I must work for, strive for, and earn. A gift is given with no strings attached. I have in my possession some championship rings, trophies, and paraphernalia that I earned as a football player through hard work. I had to sweat, ache, and even bleed to earn these awards and accolades.

Recently at Christmas, my wife and children wrapped up Christmas gifts with my name on them and placed them under our tree. I know I am over forty years old, but I still love presents. I opened those gifts of love and received them in love. I did not have to earn them; they were given to me, and I received them.

The language of man-made religion will always tilt to the necessary value man thinks they can add to salvation to obtain heaven. Here is some good news for all: Salvation is not obtained; it is received. Salvation is not earned; it is accepted. Salvation is not something we have to wish for; it is something we can possess right now because of the grace of God.

This is where we begin to understand what the real purpose of heavenly language is. Heavenly language forces one to look in the mirror of their own soul and ask themselves this simple question: "Where will I go when I die?" Heavenly language takes generic worldwide religion for all and makes us assume personal responsibility for what Jesus did for us.

It is comprehending that as I have physical parents and a physical birthday on this physical planet we call earth, I must have a spiritual birthday because God is a spiritual being, and heaven is a spiritual place. Heavenly language is honest enough to tell us we are sinners and we have transgressed God's law.

Heavenly language is honest enough to tell us that we are under condemnation. Heavenly language is loving enough to tell us there is hope. Heavenly language brings complete clarity on what Jesus brings to the table. Heavenly language tells us of His love, His mission, His purpose, His salvation, and how He personally wants a relationship with each individual.

Heavenly language leaves no doubt in the mind of a man, woman, or child the difference between religion and a relationship. Heavenly language states that man-made religion is just that—religion. Heavenly language proclaims that the spiritual birth gives us the relationship God has always desired of mankind. God is God no matter what we say. However, He is not everybody's Father. Because of our spiritual birth, God can become our Father as we become His son or daughter. Heavenly language teaches this to all.

While many look at cultural and language barriers, heavenly language sees a soul. While many see financial needs and obstacles, heavenly language sees a way. While many look at fear, heavenly language talks of faith. While many struggle with bitterness, heavenly language shines the light on forgiveness. While many criticize, heavenly language praises. While many quit, heavenly language says press on.

While many give up, heavenly language says there is hope. While many say it can't be done, heavenly language says to try one more time. While many say the home is broken, heavenly language says that God's got this. While many fail and fall, heavenly language is right there to pick them back up. While many frown their way through life, heavenly language gives away free smiles all day long. While many give up on prayer, heavenly language reminds all that the answer is just around the corner. While many cry themselves to sleep at night, heavenly language reminds us gently that the sun will come up again in the morning.

Norman, thank you for writing a heavenly language letter to my uncle Ray. Uncle Ray, thank you for signing the Gospel to my dad and my mom, using Heart Language. Most of all, Jesus, thank You for using heavenly language when talking to Nicodemus, and the woman at the well, and the young lad, and the woman of John 8, and the blind man, and me, and, well, anyone who will listen.

Heart Language is the starting point, the backbone, the runway, while heavenly language is the ultimate goal, the liftoff, and the ride. Let's do this. The world needs you, me, and our families now more than ever to speak, live, laugh, love, talk, sign, smile, and be . . . HEART LANGUAGE!

Bonus Section

Living Examples

Ye are our epistle written in our hearts, known and read of all men: Forasmuch as ye are manifestly declared to be the epistle of Christ ministered by us, written not with ink, but with the Spirit of the living God; not in tables of stone, but in fleshy tables of the heart (2 Corinthians 3:2–3).

Paul was a student and then eventually a teacher of Heart Language. Paul spent much of 1 Corinthians correcting errors, teaching doctrine, and setting things in order. By the time we read 2 Corinthians, we see an amazing change in the church. The teaching difference between the two epistles shows a difference in maturity.

The church at Corinth grew spiritually and demonstrated growth. This was made possible because Paul wrote both epistles with Heart Language. The content was different, the doctrine emphasis changed, but the spirit in which it was written was the same—Heart Language. The church at Corinth received both epistles well and responded accordingly because Paul used Heart Language.

It makes perfect sense that Paul would use Heart

Language, because as Saul when he was persecuting and slaughtering Christians, he met Jesus in Acts 9 and saw Heart Language in action. Jesus had every reason to condemn Paul and show him the error of his ways; however, Jesus was more interested in where Paul could go rather than where he had been.

That is the amazing power of Heart Language. It sees what could and should be rather than focusing on what has been. We all have faults and failures, we all have skeletons in our closet, but Jesus, with Heart Language, forgives and changes our lives.

This bonus section is intended to give us practical ideas and ways to exercise Heart Language in all of our daily lives and activities. Notice that Paul says we are known and read of all men. He also states that this reading is more than ink writing, but rather with the Spirit of God, in fleshly tables of the heart. Wait, the what? The heart!

There is that beautiful word again, the key word of this book—the heart. As we journey through this life, we can reflect on how we once were 1 Corinthian folk and are now 2 Corinthian folk, and we can help guide other 1 Corinthian folk to 2 Corinthian living.

Maybe you are reading this and still feel like you are struggling with your past. Surround yourself with the right people who use and live Heart Language, and be helped. Christianity in its purest form is modeled after its founder, Jesus. We must see the power of Heart Language and how it can change lives. So, here are some practical ways to live out Heart Language in our daily lives.

First, SMILE. Yes, it starts right here with the power of a simple smile. Smiling is one of the most contagious things we can do day in and day out. Let's take a look at the power of a good old smile. I recently asked a room full of teenagers what came to mind when they thought of the word contagious. Immediately they shared words like illness, viruses, diseases, the common cold, and the flu, and though they were right, I asked them why the word contagious always had to have a negative connotation to it. I immediately smiled, and within thirty seconds, the whole room was smiling.

When you leave your house every morning for work or school, you think about what you are going to wear. We all can relate to that. Sometimes I am casual and other times more formal, but I decided a long time ago no matter what clothes I wear, I can always wear a smile. Smiling is a simple yet powerful way for all of us to share Heart Language everywhere we go.

Make eye contact. Yes! Some of these ideas are throwback, yet they are so powerful. We live in a very different day and age, and our eyes have been so trained to look at phones and screens, we almost get nervous when we look someone in the eye. There is something special to eye contact. Talk about a difference maker. When you look someone in the eye as they talk to you, it shows that you really are listening and paying attention. My deaf family and friends are quite particular about this. Eye contact is a big deal to sign language users for obvious reasons. When you make eye contact, you use Heart Language without even saying anything.

Touch. Yes, touch. We live in a day and age where we need to be careful with this subject, and I completely understand this, but there are appropriate ways to touch. Jesus utilized the power of touch. If you spend any time with the deaf, you will learn quickly that they are far more "touchy" than the majority culture. The deaf hug more, pat shoulders and hands more, and just tend to be more touchy.

In Matthew 8, Jesus heals a leper. Jesus could have easily healed the leper by just speaking a word or two, but Jesus came close to the leper and touched him. He actually touched the leper before He said a word. The Bible never tells us how long this man was a leper, but no doubt it had been a long time since the man had felt the touch of another human due to the severity of his leprosy. Jesus made sure that before this leper was even healed, he was touched. Wow! Heart Language at its best. Hug someone today and show genuine Heart Language.

Use social media for good. Social media, already mentioned in this book, has been a breeding ground for much discouragement. People post negative things and even hateful things about people they hardly even know. If you have decided to be a Heart Language user, use social media to spread the love, encouragement, and positivity. Realize with me that life is too short. There are many hurting people in this world, and Heart Language can become a trend on social media. So whether you post, tweet, vlog, or comment on posts, use Heart Language and be a blessing.

The power of emails or texts. We all have a gold mine of Heart Language in the palm of our hand. May we use our cell phones to send quick text messages or emails such as:

"Hey. Just thinking of you and prayed for you."
"Hey friend, just wanted you to know you are loved."
"Hey, I am here for you if you need anything."
"Just wanted you to know I was thinking of you and I am so glad to call you a friend."

Messages like these can make a difference. Another way to use Heart Language:

Write letters. As a young twenty-two-year-old pastor, I asked a well-known pastor of fifty-plus years, Lee Roberson, for some tips on pastoring. One of his first responses he mentioned was to write letters with my own hand and to not type them out. For over twenty years I have done that. I have gone through hundreds of Sharpies and written thousands of letters. At the time of this writing, it still blows me away how much feedback I get from people about how refreshing it is to receive a personal handwritten note. That's right. Get out your pen, some stationery or a card, and a stamped envelope. Write away and then mail it. You will be amazed at the response you get when you use Heart Language.

Finally, say "I love you." There are so many other thoughts and ideas for how we can express Heart Language, and I already have plans for a Heart Language II that will include many ways that we can live out Heart Language on a daily basis.

On that note, I close this section with some of the most powerful words anybody can say: "I love you." Whether it is spoken in Mandarin, English, or French, or maybe written in German, Spanish, or Russian, or even signed in American Sign Language, Ecuadorian Sign Language, or Japanese sign language, these words of love will always make a difference. I do not think it is possible to say, "I love you" too much. Say it in the morning, the afternoon, the evening, and before you go to bed. If you love someone, tell them regularly, daily, and always say it with Heart Language. You see, Heart Language is understood by the Chinese child, the Englishman, the Canadian grandparent, the Japanese lady, the Spanish neighbor, the Russian teenager, the Bahamian wife, the Ecuadorian husband, and anybody with a pulse. Heart Language is for all and can be used by all. Say, "I love you."

Conclusion

World Changers

The officers answered, Never man spake like this man (
John 7:46).

We have come full circle. Allow me, first of all, to say thank you for reading this book. I started becoming a student of Heart Language early in my ministry as pastor. I have studied this language as a husband, as a father, a pastor, a son, a brother, and a friend. I fail and I fail over and over, but I can honestly testify to this simple truth—Heart Language works. There is no doubt.

We started this book by explaining that while officers were sent on a mission to arrest Jesus, they came back empty-handed, to the disappointment of the chief priests and the Pharisees. Why? Was it because Jesus had a standing army ready to defend Him? Or maybe because God made it clear that nobody was going to mess with His Son? Or maybe Jesus had some intimidating bodyguards? None of these were their reason for returning without Jesus.

They simply said, "Never man spake like this man." Their point was simple. It was not what He said, because that was the very reason they were sent. It was not that He was harassing His listeners. It was simply this: they left the presence of Jesus and were amazed at how He spoke. He was different. He mesmerized all of them.

He touched hearts with His heart. He spoke from His heart and with His heart. He looked on the crowds with love in His eyes. He made everyone feel special. Let's see, kind of like that time a deaf couple came to their son's school program knowing there would be nobody there to interpret, but they came anyway. They never said a word. They sat there smiling, not hearing one note of the music, not comprehending any of the stanzas, but they were there for their son, because they lived out Heart Language.

I often hear fitness gurus and nutritionists say that the key to good health is to make whatever diet or workout plan you have into a lifestyle. It has to become you 24/7/365. You eat right not because you are on a ninety-day diet, or a sixty-day workout, but rather, it's who you are and how you live.

May I suggest Heart Language isn't in a plan. It's not in a program. It's not something you do for a month because your church has an extra push for growth. It's not something you do only at the birthdays or anniversaries of loved ones. Heart Language is a lifestyle. Heart Language is how one lives, talks, writes, works, teaches, learns, loves, smiles, cries, laughs, and cares.

Heart Language makes the common man live in an uncommon way. Heart Language makes an ordinary person make an extraordinary difference. Heart Language is a demonstration of unforgettable behavior. Heart Language shows a dark world light, a hateful world love, a cold world warmth, a sad world happiness, a discouraged world encouragement, and a problematic world reason for praise.

Heart Language can save a marriage, restore a father and his son, draw a mother and daughter close, bond a pastor and his congregation, mend broken fences, and bridge what was once a vast gap. Finally Heart Language can bring a smile to a weeping soul.

Heart Language can and should change this world. Wherever we are in life right now—young or old, married or single, leader or follower, businessman or blue-collar worker, athlete or non-athlete, wealthy or not so wealthy—we can all apply Heart Language to our lives, which will change our lives and then change the world.

Heart Language changed my life at eight years old. I still remember this like it was yesterday. It changed my life once again ten years later at eighteen when I received Jesus Christ as my personal Savior. Though I have failed at using Heart Language sometimes, Heart Language has never failed me, and it won't fail you either.

Thank you, Dad, for always loving me with Heart Language. Thank you, Mom, for caring for me with Heart Language. Thank You, Jesus, for being the Master Teacher of Heart Language and for demonstrating this language in all that You did.

Let's go live Heart Language. Someone needs to hear you today. "Speak like never a man spake."

God bless, and use Heart Language.

About the Author

RANDY DIGNAN was born in St. Augustine, Florida, to deaf parents. He also has a younger hearing brother and a younger deaf sister. After growing up in multiple churches and being baptized several times, Randy was saved at Victory Baptist Church in Pennsylvania at the age of eighteen. He had just finished his first year of college football on scholarship after being an all-star, all-state MVP and winning two state football championships his junior and senior years of high school.

Two months after he was saved, he attended Bible College where he met the love of his life, Janelle. Janelle learned sign language and is fluent in it. They took on pastoring Bible Baptist Church while Randy was only 22 years old and not even saved four years. The church had only 28 voting members that night, and in the summer of 2005, they built a new 700 seat auditorium. God has grown the church in a miraculous way!

Randy travels nationally and internationally preaching to deaf teens, and at youth and missions conferences, and other camps and revivals. He also had a 30-minute TV program called "The Listening Heart" in English and in American Sign Language that aired four seasons worldwide weekly on CTN (Christian Television Network) and on YouTube!

He has also received two honorary doctorates, including one most recently from a Bible College in the Philippines. However, Randy's favorite part of life is being husband to Janelle and Daddy to Briella, Rayana, Grant, and Clara. His family travels with him and sings before he preaches all over the USA and in other countries. Randy loves Jesus, his family, his church, and has a special burden for the deaf and teenagers. He has a passion for the Gospel of Jesus Christ, which is evident in his preaching, and he wants all to know the Good News!

Contact Information

Facebook: Randy Dignan Heart Language; YouTube: Randy Dignan Heart Language; Instagram: @randydignan; Twitter: @randydignan

CPSIA information can be obtained
at www.ICGtesting.com
Printed in the USA
LVHW082317251020
669791LV00015B/1533